THE QUR'AN –
AN INTRODUCTION

This is the first book that deals with the Qur'anic discourse from two essential perspectives. First, the book examines the development and evolution of the concept of deity in the ancient Near East, with particular attention paid to that in the Hebrew Bible and Christology from a historical perspective. Second, the book explores the Qur'anic message from the perspective of modern knowledge.

Dr Abu-Hamdiyyah presents a distinctive, fresh and accessible introduction to the Qur'an, enabling students and the wider public to understand the various components of the Qur'an's message: the concept of God, the position of mankind in this world, the purpose of life, the guidance provided, the absolute freedom of choice, the tools needed to discern the right course in life, and finally the responsibility that goes with the freedom of choice.

Dr Abu-Hamdiyyah was Professor of Chemistry at the University of Kuwait (1973–1990). He is now retired and doing full-time research on the exposition of the Qur'anic discourse and the evolution of religion in the Near East.

THE QUR'AN – AN INTRODUCTION

Mohammad Abu-Hamdiyyah

London and New York

First published 2000
by Routledge
11 New Fetter Lane, London EC4P 4EE

Simultaneously published in the USA and Canada
by Routledge
29 West 35th Street, New York, NY 10001

Routledge is an imprint of the Taylor & Francis Group

Typeset in Garamond by Taylor & Francis Books Ltd
Printed and bound in Great Britain by St Edmundsbury – St
Edmundsbury, Suffolk

British Library Cataloguing in Publication Data
A catalogue record for this book is available from the British Library

Library of Congress Cataloging in Publication Data
The Qur'an: an introduction to its message/Mohammad Abu-
Hamdiyyah. Includes index. 1. Koran – Theology. I. Title.
BP132.A22 2000   297.1'226–dc21   99–047371

ISBN 0–415–22508–6 (hbk)
ISBN 0–415–22509–4 (pbk)

TO MY PARENTS
WHO SACRIFICED MUCH FOR MY
EDUCATION AND TO MY WIFE
JUDITH FOR HER CONTINUOUS
UNREMITTING SUPPORT

CONTENTS

PREFACE

The seeds of this study were sown more than thirty years ago when I gave a seminar about the methodology of the Qur'an to the faculty at the University of Petroleum and Minerals at Dhahran, Saudi Arabia. In 1991 I decided to enlarge the scope of my interest to cover the development and evolution of the Semitic Scriptures which originated in the Arabian Peninsula and its fertile peripheries. This necessitated not only the study of the Scriptures but also the background materials that originated in the Eastern Mediterranean region, the so-called Ancient Near East. The author found excellent treatments dealing with matters relating to and leading up to the Bible, but never going beyond that to cover the treatment of the evolution of the concept of God in the three Semitic Scriptures – the Hebrew Bible, the New Testament and the Qur'an – in a serious manner. The Qur'an, when studied, was treated separately without the proper comparative analysis emphasising the continuity of the development and evolution of the concept of God, nature of religion and revelation among the Semitic-speaking people of the Near East. Moreover, certain fundamental aspects of the Qur'an such as the nature of revelation or the stories of the previous prophets have not been satisfactorily treated before by either Muslim or non-Muslim authors.

This study aims to go some way towards remedying this situation by presenting the inspirations of Muhammad in the Qur'an as a continuation of the evolution of the concepts of God, religion and revelation that developed in the Near East. I believe the study contains significant contributions to the study of revelation in general and to that of the Qur'an in particular.

In preparing this study, I researched the major critical biblical studies written in the light of archaeological discoveries made since the nineteenth century and the recent studies on religion and revelation. I also studied the Hebrew Bible in the original tongue. This occupied my time since 1991.

In writing this, I hope to bridge the existing gap in the treatment of the evolution and development of the Scriptures that originated among the Semitic-speaking peoples of the Arabian Peninsula and its fertile periphery, provide a fresh look at the inspirations of Muhammad, and also make a contribution towards the creation of a world theology.

ACKNOWLEDGEMENTS

I am indebted to the 'Reader' for the valuable comments and constructive suggestions which helped to improve the quality of this work.

INTRODUCTORY SUMMARY

This is a new and original study on the Qur'an, the inspirations revealed to Muhammad in the seventh century CE. The study is concerned with observations on the structure (the building blocks or units) and the message of the Qur'an. It does not deal with the theological interpretations which accumulated across the ages, nor with any of the recent studies dealing with the Qur'an, but instead concentrates exclusively on the discourse of the Qur'an with the aim of examining the contents and extracting the overall plan and direction it presents. The author interacts directly with the text of the Qur'an in a straightforward objective manner to produce a fresh presentation of the Qur'anic discourse from a modern perspective.

We start first by looking at the general phenomenon in which human beings seek to understand themselves, the meaning of their existence and their relationship to the world they live in. The pictures or models humans draw for themselves based on their experiences – the observations of their social, natural and physical environments – form what were later on called 'religions' or worldviews. In this study we are mainly concerned with the worldviews which developed in the Eastern Mediterranean region, the so-called Ancient Near East, including the Hellenic and Roman civilisations. Moreover our concern is mainly focused on the development of the theistic elements in those pictures which give the perceived world its meaning, purpose and value. The general trend in the models used in pre-Scriptural and Scriptural times up to the seventh century CE is considered briefly, paying particular attention to the Bible.

The development of the concept of God as well as the main characteristic of the Hebrew Bible – the ideal of 'Israel' – which was developed by the later prophets, are discussed and the probable origins of the terms 'Israel' and of its counterpart, 'Canaan', are

1

suggested. As Christianity accepts, builds upon and modifies the main ideas of the Old Testament, the new added distinguishing and problematic feature, Christology, is considered along with two possible ideas from which it may have originally developed.

The attention of the reader is then drawn to the phenomenon of avoiding the use of 'Yhwh', the name of the God of Israel, in the translated Bibles and its replacement by 'Lord', and to the confusion which may arise from this practice. It is pointed out that the term 'Semitic' – which was coined in the eighteenth century to describe the closely related languages or dialects which arose in the Arabian Peninsula and its fertile peripheries – has an in-built contradiction. An alternative term, 'Arabaic', is recommended based on the analysis of the terms 'Arab' and 'Hebrew'. Following this is a brief look at the main developments that occurred in Mesopotamia after the rise of Christianity and prior to the appearance of Muhammad.

The interpretation of the phenomenon of 'religion' is then presented, taken from the context of the Qur'anic discourse and modern knowledge, which explains the basis for the existence of the many religions of the world. We then discuss the nature of revelation in the Qur'an. This is found to be general and serves as the basis of all knowledge, secular or religious. God reveals Himself in the creation (the world within and without the human being), not in a particular locality or in a specific period of history but at all times and at all places. The indications or signs of God are there open to all to be discerned and pursued. This is unlike revelation in the Bible, which is particularised and based on the idea that God intervenes directly miraculously (that is, against the observed laws of nature) in history. The latter creates problems, such as the justice and universality of God and the rationality and historicity of such events, thus causing a dichotomy in knowledge.

The Qur'an is then introduced and its characteristic structure set out, together with samples representing those aspects of its contents. The Qur'anic discourse addresses two situations: the general or global and the local or particular. The global platform which constitutes the framework of the Qur'anic discourse deals with the preaching of the way of God and the methodology to proceed along that way and is directed to all mankind. The particular or local aspect of the discourse deals with matters and problems that needed immediate resolution for the newly developed community, such as rituals (fasting, pilgrimage and food restrictions) and social regulations (inheritance, marriage and divorce, punishments and so on). Most of these practices were modifications of existing practices to conform to the new outlook introduced. In this study we are mainly interested in the general global framework.

Because this study is concerned with the exposition and fresh interpretation of the general framework of the Qur'anic discourse, ample space has been given to the relevant representative Qur'anic samples for illustration so that the unfamiliar reader can see them in full without referring constantly to a copy of the (translated) Qur'an. This is specially so in the sections dealing with preachings related to the ancient prophets and the preaching to the people of the Book (Christians and Jews), as these are often misunderstood by Muslims and non-Muslims alike. I have also included a relatively medium-sized surah as an appendix for a further illustration of the Qur'anic structure. In all of these illustrations of the structure of the Qur'anic framework, the author essentially lets the Qur'an speak for itself.

We then present the overall plan of the Qur'anic discourse for mankind. The most important features that emerge from this fresh look at the Qur'an are highlighted below. First, the concept of God, (1) which is a human concept that originated when mankind attained consciousness, evolves with mankind's empirical knowledge of the creation which is an ongoing activity. The way we conceive of the relationship of God to the creation, especially to mankind, is of the utmost importance for humanity because it is from this we derive our outlook on life. Second, *deen* in the Qur'an, which is usually (2) translated as 'religion', has an intrinsic meaning: the natural disposition or inborn mental orientation of seeking the truth or the way of God. This is the basis of our curiosity and the driving force for learning. Third, a methodology – observation, reasoning and ✓ (3) reflection upon the creation – is emphasised as the way to gain faith, that is, to keep us on the move and searching. This is not to prove the existence of God, which is impossible by definition, but to lead humans towards the truth (God). This methodology, once stripped of the rhetoric and the inherited religious idiom, unites the procedures of the so-called dichotomic worlds of 'science' and 'religion'. Fourth, applying the above methodology at any time (and (4) to any subject however mundane it may be) may lead to inspiration (revelation), and thus a mental picture or a model is envisioned for the reality underlying that particular subject. This study shows that, according to the Qur'an, revelation is not divided into divine and secular, but is a unified concept which derives from the same source (God).

However, since revelation is an end product of human activity in which the person involved works very hard at observing and contemplating, trying to find a picture or solution to a problem no matter how large or small it may be, the result, if one is found, may contain errors which are correctable as a result of new observations (experiences) or reflections carried out by the same person or by others at that time or at later times. The mental pictures obtained depend on the accumulated empirical knowledge at that particular time, hence the relative values of such pictures. Application of such a methodology at different times underlies the evolutionary character of such visions or models. This goes on *ad infinitum* until the end of the human mandate in this world, when finally the ultimate truth (reality) appears.

Finally, one of the most characteristic features of the Qur'anic discourse is what I call the 'politics of preaching' and the use of rhetoric and elliptical language. An example of this is the use of the inherited religious idiom in human deliberations where everything appears to be done directly by God, coupled with the simultaneous use (not necessarily in successive order) of the naturalistic language which mirrors empirical experience and human activity to describe the same event or act, such as the birth of Jesus or a human making a choice. This is done to facilitate the transition from an old non-rational position to a new rational one, thus avoiding an unnecessary confrontation and consequent alienation of the audience.

Part I

PRELIMINARY CONSIDERATIONS AND OBSERVATIONS

1

THE QUEST FOR
UNDERSTANDING OUR
WORLD

The quest for understanding ourselves and the world we live in is universal among all human beings. In this study, however, our concern will be mainly with the developments that occurred in the East Mediterranean region, especially in the Arabian Peninsula and its fertile peripheries. The East Mediterranean region is the home of the ancient civilisations of Mesopotamia, Egypt and Greece (Rome), and of the Semitic peoples and their Scriptures (the Hebrew Bible, the Gospels and the Qur'an). Several centres of civilisation formed in this region in ancient times, centres which appear on the surface to be somewhat separate but which in fact were sufficiently connected so as to allow the intimate flow of information and of people, making it possible to regard them as something of a unit. This characteristic helped keep lit the torch of seeking knowledge. When the torch was extinguished in one or more of the other neighbouring centres of civilisations, it continued to shine in the remaining ones.[1] It must be stressed, however, that the region was not completely isolated from developments in the quest for the meaning of life that occurred in other parts of the world, in particular India. We shall note some of these influences later on. In this part we are mainly interested in the evolution of the concept of the deity and its relationship with mankind up to the appearance of the Qur'an. This period will be divided into two interpenetrating eras: (1) the era preceding the appearance of the Scriptures (from ancient times up to about the beginning of the first millennium BCE when the practice of religion was predominantly based on non-exclusive worship and was mainly polytheistic); and (2) the period that witnessed the rise of the Scriptures (up to the seventh century CE). The latter period witnessed the spread of positive preaching of a particular worldview or belief (generally monotheistic) usually across communal boundaries. Compare, however, the discussion of the 'axial' period by Hick, who describes the transition state between an archial (pre-axial) period terminating at about 800 BCE and a post-axial period beginning about 200 BCE, and the fluid nature of this demarcation.[2]

Religion in pre-Scriptural times

As consciousness developed and humans became aware of themselves and their surroundings and realised how small and weak they were compared to the forces of nature, they began the struggle to make some sense of their transient existence and try to understand the world they live in. This led eventually to the development of mental pictures or models of worldviews as a result of their experiences and observations. Central to this endeavour is the postulation of a power (god) or powers that underlie all natural phenomena and which control everything in this world. Thus they looked towards those powers with awe and reverence and sought to propitiate them by ritual practices such as prayers and sacrifices to avert hardships and disasters in life, hoping they would bring abundance, happiness and peace. The universality of this phenomenon is well represented by Plutarch's remarks:

> Of all customs first and greatest is belief in gods ... [who] sanctified men, by prayers and oaths and divinations and oracles bringing them into touch with the divine in their hopes and fears. You might find communities without walls, without letters, without kings, without houses, without money, with no need of coinage, without acquaintance with theatres and gymnasia; but a community without holy rite, without a god, that uses not a prayer nor oath, nor divination, nor sacrifice to win good or avert evil, no man ever saw nor will see ... This is what holds all society together and is the foundation and buttress of all law.[3]

All sorts of objects, animate and inanimate (such as trees, stones, wells, springs, mountains, and so on), which humans thought were somehow associated with the gods and thus were described as holy, were revered and respected. People believed that the objects they idolised and adored had power and influence which could be brought into effect by performing the required rituals. This activity generated in time the practice of magic as a means to induce the gods to oblige and respond.[4]

As man's experience grew, it was realised that there were other objects beyond the earth which might be worth adoring and idolising, such as the sun, the moon and the stars. This is well illustrated in all parts of the region under consideration. Eventually man started to think in abstract terms, with the idolised objects (the deities) transcending nature, and having power over nature and society. Initially there were specialised gods and goddesses with special powers over specified natural phenomena. These gods and goddesses became personalised, on individual, tribal and national levels. For example, a tribal god was related parentally to members of the tribe as a father (or a mother for a goddess) and was responsible for their protection and guidance. Members of the tribe named themselves as the 'children or sons of [their] deity'.[5,6] Examples of addressing the gods for various reasons and how humans looked up to them are common in the literature.[7]

As tribes fought and conquered each other, forming tribal hierarchies, so the gods too became hierarchical. A good example of this phenomenon, which illustrates the intimate connection of the concepts of gods with society and thus politics, is the demotion of Seth the god of Upper Egypt and the promotion of Horus the god of Lower Egypt to chief god of all Egypt when it was unified by Lower Egypt.[8] Thus we find in all parts of this region, whether it is Semitic speaking, Egyptian or Greek (or Latin), a hierarchy of gods. For example, in Homer 'the gods are arranged on the model of a human clan, with Zeus the father of gods and of humans'.[9]

The general development and evolution of the concept of god in Mesopotamia outside the Scriptural area has been analysed by Jacobsen, who presented the data in terms of the metaphors people used for the gods. These metaphors included rulers, parents, creators and keepers of the world order as well as the personal. These representations are typical of the whole region under consideration, and have been used in all later refinements of the concept of the deity. What the ancient gods meant to their worshippers has been described by Armstrong for the Greek world,[10] but it is generally valid for the whole region.

It must be pointed out before leaving this region that in the Egyptian tradition, a sort of monotheistic concept was put forward by Akhenaten, the Pharaoh of Egypt, in the fourteenth century BCE. Akhenaten's god, Aten, the sole God, was regarded as embodied in the sun-disk, who creates and sustains life in Egypt and in foreign lands, and who is transcendent and immanent.[11] However, after Akhenaten's departure the old polytheism returned.

9

The Scriptural era

Introduction

In the first millennium BCE, Zoroastrianism came into Mesopotamia from the eastern region of Iran.[12] Zoroaster (Zarathustra) preached a new concept of God emphasising monotheism focused on Ahura Mazda (the Wise Lord), the creator of heaven and earth, day and night and light and darkness, together with a dualism. The dualism with the two opposing spirits of good and evil, who are regarded the twin children of Ahura Mazda, constitutes the basis of ethics. The beneficent and hostile spirits result from the choice they made between 'truth' and the 'lie', between 'good' and 'bad' thoughts (words or deeds) respectively. Although these concepts were soon diluted under the strong influence of Mesopotamian and Indian religions after the death of Zoroaster, they had lasting influence on religion in the area which affected the development of the Semitic Scriptures, particularly in the concepts of angels[13] and of Satan.[14]

Next we note the appearance of a religious movement in Greece called Orphism, with inspired Scriptures. Orphism's adherents believed that a human being has part of the Divine (the soul) entrapped in the human body and is doomed to transmigration if salvation is not sought.[15] To escape the cycle of reincarnation they advocated following the Orphic way of life, which includes the prohibition of eating meat, purification rituals and incantations.[16] It is apparent that this was a rejection of the sacrificial ritual which permeated all Greek culture. Some aspects of Orphism were taken up by Pythagoras and also later by Plato.

In this period, a definite tendency towards the consolidation of the various powers of different gods in one god began to appear in Mesopotamia. This is evident from the hymn of Ashurbanipal to Marduk, describing Marduk as holding the powers of the gods Anu, Enlil and Ea.[17] An even more radical text cited by Jacobsen shows that several major gods (Ninerta, Nergal, Zababa, Nabium, Sin, Shamash and Adad) are identified as but aspects of one and the same deity (Marduk). This trend tends to show a moving away from the idea of many gods with separate and specialised functions towards a simpler conception. It also shows the tendency of moving away from a deity being local, serving a particular tribe or one people, towards a deity which is universal, serving many peoples in consonance with increased knowledge and political unification tendencies.

However, periods of constant war and instability result in the brutalisation of humanity, who in turn transfer this aspect to the gods.[18] This shows again the intimate connection of the concept of the gods not only with nature but also with society and politics. This aspect has also been noted in the political struggles between two neighbouring tribes across the Jordan river in the first half of the first millennium BCE, one under Omri and his god Yhwh, the other under Mesha and his god Chamosh, as is clear from the Mesha inscription.[19]

On the whole, the consolidation of the concept of monotheism and the spread of positive preaching and campaigning for a specific worldview to the populace continued. This occurred in two characteristic ways in two different localities in the Eastern Mediterranean region. One way is general, universal, abstract and philosophical and thus elitist; it developed in several schools of thought (the Aristotelians, the Platonists, the Stoics, and so on), initially in Greece and then continuing in Roman times.[20] The divine in these philosophies is the ground of the world's being and of our own, that the world exhibits an order and system that give evidence of its divine principle, and that human beings are so designed that imitation of or likeness to a god is essential to their well-being.[21] In this approach the ordinary people, the preponderant majority, seem to have been left to their own devices, leaving them essentially untouched by the lofty ideals of these schools. Thus the general populace continued in their polytheistic practices. Ward quotes Aristotle saying 'that myths and rituals are for the artisans while the true philosopher will pursue a life of virtue and the contemplation of the most excellent of beings, the Prime Mover, in isolation from any social form of religious life'.[22] The wisdom teachers themselves more or less continued the practice of temple and civil worship as members of their local communities.[23] This is because the philosophers' account of divinity was not by intention exclusive of divine plurality: 'It was the ultimate ground of divine unity that mattered to Hellenic monotheists.'[24]

An opposite stream of thought, the school of Scepticism, appeared in the fourth century BCE, established by Pyrrho of Elis who had accompanied Alexander's expedition to India. This school of thought taught the principle of 'suspension of judgement' in order not to perturb the tranquillity of the phenomenon experienced; hence the formulas 'determine nothing' and 'assert nothing'.[25] This is another example of Indian influence, along with the idea of transmigration of souls.

The other direction or way was taken up by Semitic-speaking prophets. This was started by the 'later' Hebrew prophets in the Persian period, who preached positively the notion of a single God to arouse their people to achieve the political aim of their tribe. What is new here is the concept of positive preaching using an ideological concept of God to achieve and consolidate a political aim for one particular people.

God, the Hebrew Bible and the idea of Israel

In the Arabian Peninsula and its fertile peripheries where the Semitic-speaking peoples lived, *el* or *il* (the Akkadians used *ilu*, with the final letter indicating the sound of the nominative case ending) designated a generic Semitic name for god by the early Semites, with the probable meaning 'first' in rank and might.[26] By the time of the Ugaritic inscriptions, about the fourteenth century BCE, the chief god was also called *el* (and also *ilu*[27]). Later, the generic name became *ilh* or *elh*, pronounced *ilaah* among the Aramaeans, Hebrews and Arabs (or slightly differently according to the vocalisation in the Hebrew Bible).

In the Hebrew Bible, one may trace the evolution of the concept of God by following the names used in the Scriptures for the deity. These are *el*, the generic Semitic name for god; *elim*, the plural of *el*; *eloh*, god, which is equivalent to *ilaah* in Arabic and Aramaic and to *el*; *elohim*, the plural of *eloh*; *elohim*, taken as singular to mean god, but note both the plural and the singular senses occur sometimes in the same verse (for example, Psalm 82:1); *'the elohim'*, also taken as singular to mean god; and finally Yhwh, the God of Israel. 'Yah' is regarded as a variation of Yhwh. Elyon and Shaddai are regarded as attributes of the Deity.

The use of the plural *elohim*, 'the gods', as singular, with or without the definite article, must have started among the Semitic tribes as a short cut when talking about or addressing the gods of the different tribes in a given sanctuary, instead of naming each of them separately. This was common practice especially when making an oath or making a pledge, or visiting or passing by a sanctuary. Tolerance of worship was the rule rather than the exception which tallies with the general pieties of ancient peoples already noted above.[28] Intolerance in worship was only introduced into Israel by the prophets.[29] Separation in religious worship was introduced later after the coming of the party of the 'Exiles' to Jerusalem into power

Total misconstruction of the intent of the prophets and of the Torah.

12

under the Persian rule, as is clear from reading Ezra and Nehemiah.[30]

The coming of the 'Exiles' to power in Jerusalem marks the birth of the idea of 'Israel' as a 'holy' people, which was the moving force underlying the collection and reconstruction of the inherited Semitic narratives which became the nucleus of the Hebrew Bible.[31,32] This process somehow shifted the emphasis towards a one exclusive God instead of continuing the progression towards a universal God, glimpses of which might be detected in the Abraham narratives.[33] This is despite the fact that the idea of a One Universal God began to appear in the Persian period and was alluded to by the prophetic circles of the 'Exiles' in Mesopotamia and later in Judah itself when it became part of a province of the huge Persian Empire. Although this monotheistic idea was transferred to Yhwh,[34,35] the overall impression on reading the Hebrew Bible is that Yhwh appears mainly as a 'nationalist' God,[36] with his main concern revolving exclusively around the welfare of 'Israel'.[37] This is reinforced by passages like Deuteronomy 4:19, where it seems that other gods were assigned to other peoples and Yhwh is only for the Israelites. Furthermore, the other gods and Yhwh are being portrayed as the sons of God, as is affirmed in Psalm 89:7. Deuteronomy 32:8–9 says:

> when the most High [God] parcelled out the nations, when He spread mankind, He fixed the boundaries of peoples according to the number of the sons of God [gods]; for Yhwh's portion is his people, Jacob his allotted heritage.

The above quote, using 'the sons of God (or of the gods)' is according to the New English Bible based on the Septuagint, the Greek translation of the Hebrew Bible, which has been confirmed by a fragment of the song of Moses found at Qumran.[38] Such ideas as these compromise the concept of a 'universal' God and strict monotheism in the Hebrew Bible.

It is in this restructured material, interspersed in the Hebrew Bible, where we find the 'origin' stories containing the unethical discriminatory qualities attributed to God. These revolve around God as loving and hating arbitrarily, whether in the treatment of brothers in the same family (such as Esau and Jacob) or the treatment of two groups of Semitic-speaking people living side by side. The separation rules alienated the ordinary worshippers of Yhwh who were living normally with other Semitic peoples (the

13

Ammonites, the Ashdodites, the Samarians and the Arabians, and so on), called by the Hebrew Bible the 'peoples of the land' (for example, in Ezra 9:1 and Nehemiah 4:7) and often by the derogatory term 'Canaanites'.[39] The genesis of the religion of the district of Yehud (that is, Judaism) has been discussed recently by Davies.[40]

As a result of this restructuring, the notion of 'Israel' of biblical tradition appeared for the first time, associated with the romantic nationalist religious idea of Zion, a holy hill imagined to be in Jerusalem where Yhwh will be residing (see for example Isaiah 2:1–3, 8:18; Ezekiel 37; Jeremiah 31: 8–12; Joel 3; Obadiah, and so on). It must be pointed out that Zion is probably a corrupted form of Zephon, the holy Mount in Ugaritic literature,[41] where a dwelling place (temple) for Baal was erected in order that Baal can be on the same level as the other gods, the sons of Asherah and El. This background helps us to understand the declaration in Psalm 89:6: 'who among the sons of the gods [God] is equal to Yhwh' as Yhwh's influence overcame that of Baal.

The origin of the term 'Israel'

The term 'Israel', which is preached by the later prophets and which is the main ideal of the reconstructed Hebrew Bible, and which also forms, with little extension, a foundation for Christian theology, refers to a collective entity representing all the Jews, who are the 'son' of God.[42] We will look at all the uses of the word 'Israel' in the Hebrew Bible and examine its occurrences in extra-biblical historical texts.

The term 'Israel' in the Hebrew Bible seems to undergo changes in meaning as we go from Genesis to the later prophets. First, it is used as a substitute name for Jacob after the incident of wrestling with God (Genesis 32:29). Second, it is used in the expression 'Beni Israel', the sons of Israel, designating literally the sons of Jacob (Genesis 42:5), and later the tribes originating from the sons of Jacob (1 Kings 18:31), in other words designating a tribal name. Third, it stands for a kingdom or sheikhdom centred around the district of Samaria, in contradistinction to the sheikhdom in the district of Yehud (Judea) in the southern hills, which was populated by different tribes (see for example 2 Samuel 3:10). Finally, it stands for 'Israel' of the later prophets, which appears to convey an abstract notion generated by the prophetic circles of the 'exilic' and 'post-exilic' periods. The last meaning is associated with the idea of

Zion, the holy hill in Jerusalem, where Yhwh 'the God of Israel' would be residing. In all the above cases, 'Israel' appears in the Hebrew Bible as 'Yisrael', which is transliterated into English as Israel.

We have also the occurrence in extra-biblical historical texts of names that have been equated to 'Israel'. The oldest occurs in a Ugaritic text, reportedly as a name of a Maryano warrior. In this text (KTU 4:623 line 3) the word has been rendered as 'y(sh)ril', with the sound (sh) and not (s). In line 1 the word 'maryan' has been inferred, although the second letter is damaged and the fourth letter (n) was added by the editors. Thus if one accepts the equating of 'Israel' with 'Yshril' of this Ugaritic text, then the sound 's' in 'Israel' was originally the sound 'sh'. The second oldest mention of a name that was equated with 'Israel' occurred in the Egyptian Merneptah stele (dated thirteenth century BCE). It was rendered into English as 'Isir'il', 'Sir'il' and even 'Y(sh)r'l', and the sign on the term signified people (see below). The last rendering of the word which is equated to Israel, 'Y(sh)r'l', was given by Soggin.[43] What is of interest here is the presence of 'sh' and not 's', and the determinant of the word indicating a tribe and not a sedentary population.

Another mention is of Ahab of Israel (the kingdom or sheikhdom) by the inscriptions belonging to Salmannasar II (III?) of Assyria and which has been rendered as 'Sir'il'. It is natural to add to this list 'Shr'l', the name of a clan found in the Samarian ostraca. The name of this clan is essentially equivalent to the names given above and which were equated with the name 'Israel'. Samaria is also probably the same area implied by the other two items mentioned above, the Merneptah's stele and the Assyrian inscription. However, it is to be noted that the inscription on the ostraca starts with the sound 'sh' and not 's'. In this connection, it is of interest to point out that the extra-biblical 'Asser' has been equated to the biblical nomadic tribe 'Asher'; the sounds 'sh' and 's' are interchanged.[44] Ahlstrom gives the transliterated Egyptian inscription of the name Asher as 'isr'.[45] Again, we find the sounds 'sh' and 's' are interchanged. These inscriptions are dated around the beginning of the thirteenth century BCE. The locality of Asher was estimated to be somewhere south of Megiddo.

Taking the biblical and the extra-biblical sources together, we take the term 'Israel' as a tribal designation and the original term as the 'Beni Ishrael, i.e. sons of Ishrael'. This designation carries the characteristic imprint of the formula 'the children or sons of (their) deity' already alluded to earlier, which relates the members of the tribe to their deity. This practice was quite common among the Semitic tribes. Examples include the Beni Qais, Beni Hilal, Beni Hubal and Beni Ammon, with Qais, Hilal, Hubal and Ammo(n) being tribal deities. This is in fact a general tendency among all ancient peoples; compare for example the mythical origins of the Greeks or of the Romans.

It is obvious that 'Ishrael' is a compound word, with El forming one part. The other part is virtually self-revealing in view of the widespread worship of the goddess Asherah among the Semitic tribes, she being a goddess of fertility and also the consort of the chief Semitic deity El. According to this conjecture 'Ishrael' is related to Asherah and El, which in turn leads us to conclude that the expression 'Beni Ishrael' stands for the 'sons of Asherah and El'. The choice of the chief God and his favourite consort shows the highest degree of honour and belonging among the tribes, pointing to the high veneration paid to Asherah. One can see this in such names as 'Abd Asherti', the servant of my Asherah, in the Amarnah letters. In 'the sons of Asherah and El', the 'and' was dropped for ease of pronunciation and the sound 'sh' was later replaced by 's'. In any case, both 's' and 'sh' were written similarly in the old and the new so-called Hebrew script (and also in the old Arabic scripts) before the introduction of the distinguishing diacritical marks (which were very late indeed). In fact, in the Samaria ostraca the name of a clan was given as Shr'l (Shrael), in which the character 'sh' is given instead of the usual 's'.[46] The last reference, however, does not equate Shr'l with Israel of the Bible nor with that mentioned in the Merneptah stele.

It is in this area (Samaria) where this tribe (the sons of Asherah and El) eventually settled. The above tribal designation must have been very old, existing prior to the introduction of the worship of 'Yhwh' which spread from the south to the north. However, as the worship of Yhwh spread, the consortship of Asherah was eventually transferred to him, as is indicated by the inscriptions at Kuntillet Ajrud.[47]

The suggestion linking the tribal name 'the sons of Israel' to Asherah and El explains an outstanding problem in the 'origins' studies, namely the meaning of the original term itself. It also agrees with the abstract meaning designating the collective 'Israel' being as the son of God. The biblical explanation given to the origin of this name and what it means is not helpful and lacks real historical context. The association of Jacob and his wrestling with

God (Genesis 32:29), from which it is claimed that the name 'Israel' derives, must be regarded as part of the reconstruction of ancient traditions for ideological purposes.

The suggestion in our study also explains the competition between the worship of Asherah and Yhwh on the official level, as seen in the Hebrew Bible. On the popular level the people transferred the consortship of Asherah from El to Yhwh and continued as before the spread of Yahwism. This is supported by the large numbers of figurines found by archaeologists in the area. We must not forget that later biblical writers tried to hide or fudge certain practices which became objectionable later, such as names related to deities other than Yhwh, as is clear on reading the Hebrew Bible.

Finally, the author must draw the attention of the reader to the recent treatment of this subject by Margalith.[48] Reviewing the literature on the subject, Margalith concluded that the name should be 'Ishrael' and not Israel, taking the spelling of the Ugaritic tablet as the original one. He also rejected the usual derivation based on 'to wrestle or contend with' for the first part of the word, and suggested alternative roots based on 'to see' or 'straight'.

The origin of the term 'Canaanite'

The term 'Canaanite' is used in the Hebrew Bible in contradistinction to the term Israelite. Therefore it is of interest to enquire of the origin of this term and of the land of Canaan. Canaan is a verbal noun derived from the verb cana'a or khana'a, with 'representing the guttural sound ('ayn). Khana'a means to submit, to give up, or to lose the will to fight and resist. The subject of 'the Canaanites and their land' in historical documents and in the Hebrew Bible has been recently treated in full by Lemche.[49] What is important to point out here is that the so-called Canaanites of the ancient Near East did not call themselves Canaanites. It is a term used by others to mean essentially the occupied or subjugated people.

The term was originally used in correspondence between one power in Mesopotamia complaining to the occupying power (Egypt) about an event which occurred in the land in southwestern Asia which was under the jurisdiction of Egypt and therefore needed attention. Later the term was mentioned in the Amarnah letters, the correspondence between Egyptian vassals of the occupied lands in Syria-Palestine and the rulers of Egypt. As the extent of the occupied lands in southwestern Asia (Syria and

[handwritten margin note: etymology does not determine meaning as much as usage]

Palestine) varied according to the military circumstances of Egypt, so did the designated lands of the 'Canaanites'. The people of these occupied lands by Egypt (the so-called Canaanites) were essentially Semitic-speaking peoples, whether they were living in cities and towns or were pasturalists and partly nomadic; these people may also have had different dialects depending on their lifestyles.

Lemche, in his monograph on the Canaanites, points out that: 'Only in the Hellenistic period at the end of the first millennium BCE may we speak of a certain and fixed idea among the peoples of the ancient Near East as to the location of Canaan, because of the identification of Canaan with Phoenicia.'[50] All this, it must be stressed, is dependent on accepting the equivalence of the terms used in the ancient documents (inscriptions) with the terms used in the Hebrew Bible for Canaan and Canaanites, and this is not a straightforward matter.

Transition to Christianity

After the time of Ezra and Nehemiah, a doctrine was adopted by the rabbis that 'The Holy Spirit' departed from 'Israel' and no more prophetic inspirations were forthcoming;[51] hence Haggai, Zechariah and Malachi were the last of the prophets in the Hebrew Bible. The closing of the door of prophecy opened the door for a new type of literature to appear. Some of this literature was included in the Hebrew Bible not under the 'prophets' but under the category of 'writings'. Under the latter heading appeared the books of Job and Qohelet, completely abandoning the usual discourse where God's concern is made exclusively to revolve around 'Israel'. The former book tends to say there is no special relationship with God and that what happens to humans in this world is arbitrary, with no connection to their behaviour, and may only be a result of a bet between God and Satan. The latter book is also sceptical about life, stressing its meaninglessness and the futility of pursuing anything worthwhile, reminiscent of the fatalism and hedonism of some of the pre-Islamic Arabian poets. In fact, it seems that reference to God completely disappears in the book of Esther, another book in the 'writings' category in the Hebrew Bible. It is clear from the text of this book, and the fact that it was included in the canonical Scriptures, that the discourse of religion at the time the book was composed was reduced to simple lobbying at the royal court of the imperial power of the time. This again shows the intimate connection between religion

[handwritten margin notes: ? ?< SP !]

[handwritten note at bottom: of course! the question is. what is the connection?]

and politics (society). Thus from about the first or second century CE, the time the contents of the Hebrew Bible were fixed, all religious efforts were concentrated and directed towards interpreting the Holy Book and its preservation and transmission.

During the Persian and Hellenistic periods, the concept of angels started to appear as soon as the idea of 'One God Only' started to take root. Instead of the lesser gods carrying out certain functions in the natural world, we now have messengers or 'angels' of God doing the job. In the Hellenistic era, the idea of messianism also developed as a reaction to the state of affairs that prevailed among the Jewish community, who were hoping for an anointed saviour (usually a king) to appear to save 'Israel'. Eventually Jesus appeared on the scene, which was already witnessing a lot of political and religious activity. In this turbulent environment, Jesus began to preach to the Jews about the kingdom of God; however, he was rejected by the Jewish religious establishment in Jerusalem.

The stories about the life of Jesus and his sayings were taken up by his disciples and followers, who later transmitted what they heard and learned. Some of these stories and sayings may be seen in the four canonical gospels in the New Testament, and also in the recently discovered gospel of Thomas. There appears to be a difference in emphasis in these two collections on the method of salvation. The salvation proclaimed in the gospel of Thomas is based on self-reliance and self-discovery, with no discussion of Jesus's suffering, death and resurrection. The other four gospels of the New Testament offer simply salvation through Christ.[52] In the gospel of Thomas, Jesus preaches 'the kingdom is inside of you ... when you get acquainted with yourselves ... you will understand that it is you who are children of the living Father'.[53] Christianity as it is known today is based on the Christ of faith and not the Jesus of history. The shift from following the teachings of Jesus as an inspired person to that of the mythological Christ is well described by Mack.[54]

Possible origins of Christology

Christianity was born when Paul (a Jewish rabbi with the Hebrew name Saul) adapted the message of Jesus by shifting the emphasis from preaching to the Jews to preaching to the non-Jews (the gentiles, mainly the non-Jewish Semitic elements forming the major part of the population in the area), and by developing Christology. The latter may have been an adaptation of the concept of a triad used in worship in 'Arabia' (see below). Paul, in Galatians 1:16–17, stressed that before he embarked on his mission he did not confer with flesh and blood, nor did he go up to Jerusalem to confer with the apostles, but he went into Arabia before returning to Damascus. Although some districts in Mesopotamia and the Nile Delta were sometimes called by the name Arabia, the Arabia which was mentioned by Paul in Galatians probably meant the land of the Nabataeans.[55] This Arabia had its centre at Petra, but its influence extended north to Damascus, south to Yathrib (Medina) and beyond and west to the Sinai Peninsula, Gaza, and along the sea coast.[56, 57]

The main deity worshipped in Petra was Du'l-Shara, together with a goddess who was regarded as his mother.[58] Du'l-Shara was represented by a block of stone, which served also as the deity's abode and seat of power. As Du'l-Shara means 'He of Shara' and Yhwh 'He of Sinai' (also of Seir, or of Edom (Judges 5:4–5)), it has been pointed out that Yhwh, like Du'l-Shara, inhabited a rock called Beth El (the house of God).[59] If we remember that Seir, Edom and Shara, Nebo,[60] Teman[61] and probably Sinai are all in the same area and, coupled with the widespread belief that the deity resided at top of mountains,[62] it is not improbable that both deities (Du Sinai, or 'Yhwh', and Du'l-Shara) had common origin in the area and might be identical. Could it be then that a sort of a triad in the form of God (*el*), the Father, the Son (Yhwh, Du'l-Shara) and the holy spirit, a mother goddess (al-Lat, han-Ilat, or Asherah) was developing and beginning to be used, if not already established, in worship? This does not appear far-fetched in view of the bits of information embedded in the Hebrew Bible[63] and also from information derived from inscriptions in Southern Arabia.[64]

Christology may also have been an adaptation of the main idea in the Hebrew Bible, that 'Israel', a collective entity representing all the Jews, is the 'son' of God.[65] The 'election' is thus transferred to a single person (Jesus). When this is coupled with the prediction that the Saviour of 'Israel' will be born of a virgin,[66] the latter would constitute the third component of the triad, the holy spirit. The idea of the holy spirit being connected with a goddess of fertility is well entrenched in the ancient Semitic belief.[67] Moreover, the recent discoveries of inscriptions at Kuntillet Ajrud in Sinai pointing to Yhwh having a consort, the goddess Asherah, tend to confirm this.[68] This aspect of Yhwh (having Asherah as a consort) must have been transferred to him after the worship of Yhwh became dominant over the worship of Baal. In view of the

what utter nonsense and rampant speculation,

20

widespread popularity of Asherah, as was suggested earlier, her name probably forms part of the name 'Israel'. The idea of a dying god and the involvement of a goddess of fertility in the annual celebrations is well attested in the Semitic literature, and its practice was widespread in the fertile peripheries of the Arabian desert, so much so that we find it practised even in the Temple in Jerusalem (Ezekiel 8:14).

In the very early stages of primitive Christianity, Paul addressed the poor non-Jewish Semitic population (for example, in Galatians 1:21–23) in towns in Aramaic or colloquial Greek, apparently not in the literary Greek. It was only later generations of Christian missionaries who introduced philosophical sophistication in preaching and adapted some well-known Greek philosophical concepts, especially the very descriptive expression 'Spermaticosa Logos' to describe Christ. (For more about the sort of Greek language used by Paul and for the continuity of the new discourse with the existing culture of the so-called pagan population of the Near East, see the work of Deissmann.[69])

Christianity was born to remedy the exclusiveness of Judaism by inviting all other peoples of the world into the fold. However, it made the idea of one God more complex by adopting the idea of the 'son of God' appearing as man on earth, the crucifixion and the resurrection as an act of redemption for what is called the original sin of man. Additionally, it made the priesthood (the Church) an intermediary between man and God. However, early 'non-orthodox' Christians did in fact oppose the introduction of the 'Church' with its hierarchical structure, as can be seen in the writings of the early Christian fathers against heretics.[70] Some of the ideas and beliefs outside the canonical Scriptures can be seen in the apocryphal and pseudepigraphical literature.[71,72] In fact the recent discoveries at Qumran[73] and at Nag Hammadi[74] tend to show alternative interpretations of the Jesus message, and for some of the main Qumran writings an alternative for the Torah as well.[75]

The name Yhwh in the translated bibles

Before leaving the subject of God in the Bible, it is interesting to point out a certain development or discontinuity which arose concerning the use of the name Yhwh outside the Hebrew Bible. This apparently started first when the Bible was translated into Greek and later into other languages. In Greek, Latin, Arabic or English (and presumably other languages), Yhwh, God of Israel,

Utterly wrong

appears as 'Lord'. *Lord* is an epithet, not a name. It is not our intention to argue here against the use of this epithet to describe Yhwh, which is of course proper and legitimate, but to argue against equating it with the name Yhwh and thus replacing Yhwh when standing alone in a text with 'Lord'. In effect, Yhwh disappears from the translated text with no other 'name' taking its place. Yhwh does not literally mean lord.

Thus we have in the English Bible an epithet of the deity being used instead of the name Yhwh, which we find in the Hebrew Bible. It is true that (late) Jewish practice considered Yhwh too sacred to pronounce, and so *'the name'* was used instead of Yhwh in ordinary speech, but the use of Yhwh continued in written form. However, the written form is vocalised to sound like 'Adonai', which means 'my master' or 'my lord'. This apparent complete shunning of the use of Yhwh, the name of the God of Israel, in the translated Bibles and the avoidance of even its translation into an equivalent 'name' when standing alone in the text, is perplexing. It looks like an undeclared veto against the use of the name Yhwh outside the Hebrew Bible. This practice created a discontinuity and confusion between the Old and New Testament, as Christ is also called 'Lord' in the New Testament. This usage in the New Testament may sometimes create confusion. For example, Acts 4:26 says: 'The kings of the earth ... gather together against the Lord and against his Christ.' Note the Hebrew translation of this verse gives Yhwh for 'Lord'.[76]

Further confusion and inconsistency arises because 'Lord' as an epithet (in the form of Adonai) is sometimes (rightly) used along with Yhwh in the Hebrew Bible, for example in Isaiah 40:10, Ezekiel 2:4, 3:11, and so on. Thus we have for 'Adoni Yhwh' in the Hebrew Bible the translation 'Lord God' in King James's Version and the New English Bible, and 'Sovereign Lord' in the New International Version. In the former translation, 'Lord' rightly stands for Adonai (although they miss the possessive pronoun at the end of Adon) and God for Yhwh. In the latter translation, the possessive pronoun is also missed and two epithets, Sovereign and Lord, have been used for what ought to have been 'my lord Yhwh'. Note the confusion one finds in the translation of Malachi 3:1, where we have 'Lord' standing rightly for Adon but also 'Lord' standing for Yhwh. As this practice was apparently started with the translation of the Hebrew Bible into Greek in the third or second century BCE and which was continued later in the Latin and other versions,[77] one can only surmise that the name Yhwh was not suitable for non-Jewish readers and so its use was evaded. For Christians, this practice was perhaps adopted to avoid the literal conclusion that Christ was the son of Yhwh; or perhaps it was the inability to fit Yhwh in the trinity of Father, Son and Holy Spirit. It is interesting to note in this connection the gnostic Christians' accusation that the orthodox Christians worshipped an image of God, not the true God, and that this God, the god of Israel, must be different from that of the forgiving God of Jesus.[78]

It is well to remember that the last words of Jesus on the cross were reported to be, 'my God, my God, why have you forsaken me?' (Matthew 27:46), in which Jesus uses the generic Semitic name for the deity, *el*, and not Yhwh. It is to be noted that in the Semitic tongue there are no capital letters, so *el* and *El* are written similarly.

Transition towards the Qur'an

The early Christian period was alive with new ideas and interpretations which were preached and argued in the whole region, especially in Mesopotamia where Persian ideas of dualism were well established alongside many varieties of gnostic ideas, Buddhism, and Greek philosophies. Such activities led to the formation of two religions, Mandaeanism and Manichaeanism, and to modifications of Zoroastrianism in the Sassanid period.

Mandaeanism and Manichaeanism are universal, gnostic and dualistic teachings which use elaborate gnostic mythological structures to picture or symbolise the powers contending for the control of the world. In the fight between the realm of Light (Spirit) against the realm of Evil or Darkness (matter), interpenetration (mixing) occurs. The aim of these teachings in this life is the separation of these two components from each other and the return of the Spirit to its origin, the realm of Light. A general framework for the structure of the gnostic myth in the pseudepigraphical 'Christian' literature is discussed by Layton.[79]

In Mandaeanism, according to Buckley,[80] the two realms contending for control of human destiny are the upper heavenly realm and the underworld or the lower realm. In the upper realm there is a pre-existing primary entity called 'the Great Life', or 'Lightworld', who resides with his consort 'Treasure of Life', together with many Lightbeings. The earthly world and human beings are not created by the Primary Lightworld entity but by a Lightbeing who previously fetched back the Spirit from the underworld because of its necessity for life on earth. Because the creation was wholly material, man could not stand erect, so a *soul* is brought from the Lightworld to function as a revealer and make man complete so that he can stand erect. With the human being now made complete, he is taught to free his soul and spirit by the primary saviour and messenger (Manda d-Hiia or knowledge of life), and to return to the Lightworld origin, leaving his body behind. The priests in this religion mediate between the upper realm and humans and are regarded in this capacity as Lightbeings.

What is also of interest is that this religion originated from the teachings of John the Baptist, and that the origins of the Mandaeans can be traced to the second or third century of the common era when they emigrated from the Jordan Valley area eastwards, eventually settling in southern Babylonia. The name given in the Ginza (the holy book of the Mandaeans) for John the Baptist is Yahya, which is the same name given in the Qur'an. Because of this, Buckley suggested that this part of the Ginza, Right Ginza 7, was written in the seventh century CE.[81] However, in view of the use of the descriptive terms – 'the Great Life' for the primary entity in the upper heavenly realm, 'Treasure of Life' for his consort, and 'Knowledge of Life' for the primary saviour and Messenger, and assuming that these terms were all used before the coming of Muhammad – it is not far-fetched to consider Yahya as the original name (or epithet) of their prophet. This is because 'Yahya' means 'to live', or 'he lives', from which the noun 'hiia' (life) is derived. Moreover 'John' has a different etymology.

Manichaeism, a universal and strongly dualistic religion, was revealed to and preached by Mani in the third century CE in Babylonia and other neighbouring civilisation centres as far as India. Mani declared himself the 'messenger of God come to Babylon', the 'Seal of the Prophets' and 'the apostle of light' in whom the Paraclete was incarnated to provide salvation and hope for the whole of suffering humanity.[82] Two irreducible opposites or principles are conceived, personified as the Father of Greatness and the Prince of Darkness. The cosmic history is divided into three stages. In the first, the two irreducible opposites were separate, residing respectively in the north and in the south, kept apart by a border between their two kingdoms. The second stage, the present age, is initiated when the Prince of Darkness penetrates the kingdom of the Father of Greatness. During the struggle that ensued – involving what Gnoli terms repugnant acts of cannibalism and sexual practices as well as the self-destructiveness and autophagia of matter – heaven and earth, beasts and plants and finally Adam and Eve were created. In the second stage, the Prince of Darkness encourages procreation in order to create more and more corporeal prisons to entrap the element of light, while salvation is achieved by liberating light from its entrapment in matter by interrupting the cycle of reincarnation through the retention of the sperm and through rigorous asceticism and knowledge. When the church of justice triumphs (the third stage), the future begins and the souls will be judged; those of the chosen will rise to heaven. The world will then be purified and destroyed with a fire, and matter, in all its manifestations and with its victims (the damned), will be forever imprisoned in a globe inside a gigantic pit covered with a stone, thus accomplishing the separation of the two principles forever.

This religion looks upon life in a very pessimistic manner. In fact life is looked upon as if an error was committed which must be rectified by separating the soul and spirit from the body (matter), the latter taken to represent evil. Since the two contending principles are irreducible and coeval, the concept of One God as the Ultimate in this world is not clear. It is of interest to note that in this religion the concept of light as a seed, as in the Greek term 'Spermaticosa Logos', was adopted and put into practice literally in the Manichaeism mythology.

As already stated earlier,[83] Zarathustra preached the concept of One God, the Wise Lord, the creator of the whole world. He also proposed two opposing principles, as twin children of the Wise Lord, to explain the good and evil tendencies in human beings. This message, however, was soon diluted and by the time of the Achaemenides some pagan gods (the ones worthy of worship) were reabsorbed from the Indo-Iranian pantheon and from the surrounding cultures in Mesopotamia such as Mithra, Anahita, Vayu, the sun, the moon, and so on. Eventually the Wise Lord became the Supreme God, not the only God. In later evolution of this religion, under the influence of Hellenism (especially the notion of Fate) and of Babylonian astronomy, Ahura-Mazda was demoted further. He was no longer considered as the transcending principle but was set against the principle of evil, forming a twin offspring of a higher force, namely Time or Zurfan.[84,85]

All these cross-currents of ideas about the meaning and purpose of life – pagan and otherwise – were circulating in the Near East, whether in written or oral form, and must have been known in the seventh century at the time of Muhammad, judging from certain verses of the Qur'an concerning the crucifixion of Jesus among other things. The pantheon in Arabia, which continued in existence side by side with Christianity, Judaism and some other forms of monotheistic tendencies until Muhammad's time, consisted of gods and goddesses who were worshipped to bring the worshippers nearer to 'Allah', the God. All these various deities have been discussed by Fahd in relation to the religious practices of the Semites in the Arabian Peninsula at large.[86]

In the midst of this Semitic milieu, which had been cross-fertilised by all sorts of ideas, and in the centre of the Arabian Peninsula, separated but not isolated, there came Muhammad preaching that there is only One God for all creation, *Allah* (an assimilated form of *Al-ilaah*, the god), with no other gods besides Him, accessible to all, with no priesthood as an intermediary, no original sin and no ethnic, tribal or racial overtones. In the Qur'an we find God addressing human beings in general or the believers, but never 'the Arabs' or 'men' in contradistinction to 'women'.

Muhammad preached an integrated universal plan directed to all mankind, in which authority on earth is devolved to mankind with the creation at their disposal to utilise. They are given the tools of learning (inspiration or revelation) and the general guidelines to be used in order to stay on the right course, as well as the freedom to choose. Muhammad preached that this life is a trial period for humanity, the latter being recognised as made up of different tribes and nations of various colours and tongues, and gave the basic formula for peaceful coexistence among the various nations and communities. The preaching revolved around the central theme that after death every body will be raised at the Day of Judgement and all will be judged by God based on their conduct in this life. As will be seen later, Muhammad's inspirations put mankind on a new footing by stressing the use of empirical observations and the use of reason and reflection as the guiding tools for seeking the way of God.

The term 'Semitic'

Before proceeding to discuss the interpretation of religion and revelation, we will comment on the term 'Semitic', which is used quite often when discussing the people, religions and languages of the Arabian Peninsula and its fertile peripheries. The term 'Semitic' was coined to describe a group of closely related languages spoken in the Arabian Peninsula and its fertile periphery. This attribute is based on the name 'Shem' or 'Sem' found in the Bible. The Bible gives names of nations which descended from Shem who were not among the 'Semitic'-speaking people and vice versa; in other words, nations not descending from Shem were Semitic-speaking. Thus the term 'Semitic' in the Bible pertains to political and not linguistic considerations.[87] We prefer instead the term 'Arabaic' over 'Semitic' because the latter term has a built-in contradiction.

The term 'Arabaic' may be shown to reflect two important characteristics, one relating to lifestyle and the other to language. 'Lifestyle' refers to the state of roaming or the state of being continually on the move, as seen by a sedentary observer. The words 'Hebrew' and 'Arab' are derived from the verbs *'abara* and *'araba*, which mean to cross (a desert, a district, a river) or pass by (a community, a town), and to disappear (temporarily, like the sun setting) or pass by quickly and then appear again, respectively. The latter meaning for *'araba* may be contested lexicographically, but it is the meaning which makes sense to this author's 'Semitic' ears. Both *'abara* and *'araba* seem to convey the same sense and may have been used simultaneously in the early development of the language. The uttering of words to give a certain meaning is based on sound. Similar-sounding utterings of verbs were used to convey a spectrum of actions which are of similar nature. For example, the verb *gharaba* means to set (for the sun) or to move away (for a person). Another verb, *'azaba*, meaning to depart, leave or move away, appears both in the Hebrew Bible (for example, Genesis 24:27) and in the Qur'an (for example, 10:61) in the same sense. When writing was initially developed using only consonants, all these similarly uttered verbs (they all start with guttural sounds) were written in the same way. Later, differentiation was introduced to stress certain shades of action. This differentiation was finally established by the invention of the diacritical marks.

In the case of *'abara* and *'araba*, both are based on the same three letters (the guttural represented by the first letter, 'ain, in both words, and the two consonants b and r) with the second and third consonants interchanged. This sort of interchange is quite common in this family of languages. Both of these verbs give the same shade of meaning one gets from *gharaba*. The latter verb was initially written exactly the same as *'araba* and *'azaba*, but now they are distinguished from each other by diacritical marks. It is also worth noting that the Hebrew Bible preserved words based on the letters 'rb (again, the first letter is guttural) which give the two meanings — Arab and sunset — if we ignore the different vocalisations given.

The Masoretic vocalisation was very late, and possibly was done arbitrarily in order to differentiate the words.

The active participles of *'abara* and *'araba* are *'aabiru* and *'aaribu* respectively. It is from these two nouns we get *'Ibri* and *'Arabi*, meaning pertaining to (an) *'aabiru* and to (an) *'aaribu*, respectively, which stand for 'Hebrew' and 'Arab' respectively after shortening the words for ease of pronunciation. Of course when this state of 'being on the move' no longer holds for some people (in other words, they become settled), they will be known by a tribal name or by a name derived from the name of the place they settled in, or by any other adopted name. It is of interest to point out that the attribute of being 'on the move' (*'aabiru* or *'aaribu* (Hebrew or Arab)) originates from the settled population who observe the goings and comings of people with such lifestyle. Both the settled and those 'on the move' here speak essentially the same language. This custom of nomenclature, sedentary or settled and 'Arab', continued right down to the present. Before leaving the subject of lifestyle, it is also pertinent in this connection to draw the attention of the reader to the way the Egyptian Nilotic society described people of such lifestyle. They used a verb meaning 'moving on foot' or denoting 'the daily motion of the sun', in effect reinforcing the above meaning suggested for *'araba*.[88]

The other aspect which makes the use of 'Arabaic' more appropriate than 'Semitic' is linguistically based. As pointed out by Mendenhall,[89,90] the Arabic language preserved the basic framework of the proto-language better than any of its sister dialects. Thus the term 'Arabaic', which conveys a linguistic sense as well as a sense of a lifestyle, might be a better descriptive term for the group of closely related languages which were spoken in the Arabian Peninsula and its fertile peripheries in ancient times.

2

INTERPRETATION OF THE CONCEPTS 'RELIGION' AND 'REVELATION'

The history of the term 'religion'

The worship of the gods (or God) which is usually associated with the practice of rituals is now described by the well-established term 'religion'. Smith has comprehensively analysed the origin of this term and its use in history.[1] The term is based on the Latin term *religio*, which was used in pagan Roman times to designate 'the power outside man obligating him to certain behaviour under the pain of threatened retribution' or to describe 'the feeling in man vis-à-vis such powers', with the ritual ceremonies themselves called *'religiones'*. Smith traced the evolution of the use of the terms *religio* and *religiones* from pagan times up to the modern era. By the fifth century CE, the time when the Church's triumph over paganism was complete, there is a noticeable change in meaning, moving from the general to the specific. For example, Smith cites Lucretius (in *De Rerum Natura*) and Cicero (in *De Natura Deorum*) using the term *religio* generally; the former welcomes scientific materialism in order to liberate man from *religio*, referring to the ceremonies used in the worship of the gods, and the latter speculates on the nature of the gods, the divine. On the other hand, Augustine in the fifth century CE, in his famous book *De Vera Religione*, says that 'true religion means the worship of the one true God, that is, the Trinity, Father, Son and Holy Spirit'.[2]

In Christendom in the Middle Ages, *religio* mostly designated life in monasteries and such orders. However, Aquinas in the thirteenth century, when the Mediterranean basin had become a melting pot of interaction of Muslim and Christian thought, used the term *religio* in more than one sense, to designate the outward expression of faith, the inner motivation towards worshipping God and the worship itself, and the bond that unites the soul with God. These aspects, especially the latter, are of particular interest to us in this study. Aquinas spoke of the creature having become – by creation – in a sense separated from his original existence in God, and quoted Augustine as saying '*religio* reunites us to the one almighty God'. He goes on to say that *religio* first rebinds man to God by faith and fitting worship, pointing out that every Christian at his baptism partakes of true *religio*. Second, *religio* is the obligation whereby a man binds himself to serve God in a particular manner, by specified works of charity and by renunciation of the world.[3] A little later, at the beginning of the Renaissance in the last quarter of the fifteenth century, Ficino (a translator of the works of Plato and of Plotinus) used *religio* to designate an innate, natural and primary universal human characteristic, a divinely provided instinct that makes man man, by which he perceives and worships God. Moreover, Ficino stresses that 'all opinions of men, all their responses, all their customs, change – except *religio*'.[4] It is clear that *religio* here stands for an inner driving force for the worship of God and not for external manifestations such as rituals and laws (see *fitratu Allah* below).

In the Reformation period, it was a rebellion against the Catholic Church that dominated the discussion of *religio*, especially the terms false and true *religio* within Christianity. In the Enlightenment period the discussion centred around the idea of religion being natural to man achievable by reason alone. In this period the idea of contrasting 'natural' with 'revealed' religion was born. Smith notes that this was the first time the term 'revealed religion' has been used, pointing out that although revelations were not new to the Bible thinking, no one before the eighteenth century had supposed that what was revealed was a religion.

The idea that 'religion' describes a universal human activity, as a result of which we have the various religions such as Christianity, Judaism, Buddhism, Hinduism, Islam, and so on, is now well established, although some Christian theologians still refuse to accept such description because of the fear of relativisation. Smith points out in his comprehensive study of the use of the term 'religion' that it has no counterpart in Mesopotamian, Greek, Egyptian or the Eastern civilisations, nor is it to be found in the Bible or other world Scriptures except in the Qur'an (of the seventh century CE). This is explained by Smith as being due to the special position of the Near East between the East and the West and the involvement of the area and the people of the area with the totality of world history which 'seem to make incipiently possible a unified view of man's religious history on a world scale'.[5] The Qur'an also, Smith points out, gives a descriptive characteristic name for the religion preached within its pages, unlike the names of the other religions of the world whose names (Buddhism, Christianity, Judaism, Hinduism, and so on) were given to them by outsiders. So what does the Qur'an say about 'religion'?

Religion in the Qur'an

The word which stands for 'religion' in the Qur'an is *deen*. The word *deen*, which occurs ninety-one times in the Qur'an, carries several shades of meanings. For example, in 109:3 it indicates a generic name for religion, way, direction or outlook on life. In 30:30 or 42:13, it occurs with the definite article to indicate 'the upright religion', the right way or the straight path, as in 1:6. This is further explained in 3:19 by saying that 'the religion' is the total commitment (usually translated as surrender) to the way of God. In 1:4, 'the day of the *deen*' means the day of judgement or of reckoning. In 7:29 or 39:3, *deen* with the definite article means total devotion or allegiance.

The word *deen* is derived from the verb *daana* (originally *dayana*) which means to give on credit (to loan), to profess or acknowledge allegiance (gratitude), or to judge. This verb is also the root of *dayn*, which means debt or obligation and which occurs in the Qur'an five times. There are two verbal usages of *daana* in the Qur'an, one an imperfect of *daana* (*yadeenoona*) used with *deen* as an object (9:29) with the meaning 'to follow, to profess or to acknowledge'; the other usage is *tadaayantum* (2:282), which is the reciprocal form of *daana* (*dayana*), with the meaning of 'transacted on credit'. There are two usages of a past participle: *madeenoon*, in 37:53, with the contextual meaning of 'to be judged', and *madeeneen*, in 56:86, with the contextual meaning of 'owing' or 'dependent'. It appears at first glance that the verb *daana* gives rise to two independent nouns with entirely different meanings, namely: *dayn* (debt) and *deen* (religion, way or direction). These two words are written exactly the same without vocalisation, but somehow came to be pronounced differently, with the sound 'ay' changing to 'ee' to differentiate it from the other usage. This sort of change is also seen in ordinary spoken urban Arabic, for example 'kayf(a)', which means 'in what manner', has become 'kaif' or 'keef'. However, on closer scrutiny one notices a merging of the two meanings. This merging seems to occur in 24:25 where the verb *waffaa*, which means to fulfil a promise (or an obligation) or to pay a debt in full, is used with *deen* as its object to give the meaning 'to pay them their just due in full', as if *deen* is taken as *dayn*. The two meanings of *dayn* and *deen* merge also in the idea of giving an account of something given to a person, in one case money (or something equivalent), in the other the gift of life, the apparatus of living and thinking. The Day of Judgement in the former case is the date when the debt is due to be paid; in the latter it is the day when one gives account of what one has done with one's life, the credits and debits collected along the way in life.

One gets the impression of being in debt to God in many verses of the Qur'an. An example is the following:

> Has there [not] been a [long] span of time before the human being [appeared] during which he was not anything worth remembering (mentioning)? We have created the human being from a sperm-drop, a mingling, so that We may put him to the test, thus We made him a discerning being endowed with hearing and seeing. Indeed We have shown him the way [and it rests with him to be] either grateful or ungrateful.
>
> (76:1–3)

Another example is 16:78:

> And God has brought you forth from your mothers' wombs knowing nothing – but He has endowed you with hearing and sights and minds so that you may have cause to be grateful.

Many other examples can be seen dispersed in the Qur'an, all of which contrast the giving of the necessary apparatus of life for discerning with the human response (gratitude or lack of it) to such a gift. We are told that what we are given is a sort of trust for us to use along the way of life, and that we will have to give account of its use (17:36). This constitutes the source of indebtedness to God, and this interpretation is confirmed by the use in the tradition of the expression 'the Dayyaan' as an attribute of God. The root verb for *dayyaan* is *dayyana* which is the intensive form of the verb *daana* (*dayana*).

What is implied in the above is that human beings are given the gift of discernment, and they have the choice of being either grateful or ungrateful. This is a basic principle in the Qur'an, and is at the heart of its message which forms the basis of human responsibility and hence judgement. The apparatus of observation, reasoning and reflection is used for discerning the right direction or way leading towards God.

The concept of *deen* in the Qur'an was also discussed by Gardet,[6] who essentially arrives at conclusions similar to those above regarding the intimate connection between *deen* and *dayn*. However, Gardet in his analysis seems to stress that the 'owing, debt or obligation' concerns mainly the rituals or cult, emphasising that the latter is the essential part of *deen*, citing the association by Muslim authors of *'ibaadaat* – the acts of service' and *deen*. However, this restriction or limitation imposed on the acts of service cannot be right as can be seen from the verses of the Qur'an. For example, 2:177 (quoted later), which best summarises what I call 'the creed of Islam', stresses against taking pure 'ritualism' as an act of righteousness and then goes on to specify the righteous actions for a believer, emphasising many things which are not cultic.

Gardet also dismisses the suggestions that the word *deen* was taken from the Pahlevi *den*, pointing out that the Mazdaic religion is different from the religion of Islam. In this study, we stress the continuity and the common basis of the Semitic languages, as has been recently propounded by Buccellati,[7] which makes the Mazdaic *den* (*dain*) more likely to be a loan word from Semitic.

The word *deen* occurs in the Qur'an only in the singular, but allows for more than one *deen* (way or religion), depending on the human choices and their deliberations. But the Qur'an specifically states that there is only one upright way (religion), the straight way, which is described below. How can one, then, recognise this way? Only through the use of the apparatus provided involving observation (experience), reasoning and reflection.

In order to elucidate further the basis of following the right way (that is, the right religion) we must consider the basic tendency or instinct which the Qur'an calls *fitratu Allah* with which God initiated human beings in the first instance. This is given in 30:30 below, where Muhammad is instructed to set his direction (face) towards the right way, the natural way with which God originated human beings:

> So set your face (direction), inclining towards 'the deen' (the religion or way): God's original creation upon which He originated (disposed) mankind. There is no changing to God's creation. That is the upright religion (way) but most people do not know.

It is stressed that this is part of the creation in which humanity was born (or broken) into and cannot be changed; it is part and parcel of human nature, the driving force behind our inquisitiveness and enquiry. This is more general than the natural religiousness of the Enlightenment.[8] The verb *fatara*, with its verbal noun *fitrah*, both of which are used in the above verse, gives us the impression that religion would spring out of humanity like a new growth from a germinating seed breaking (or cleaving) the surface of the soil seeking light (compare this with Spermaticosa Logos of the Stoics). (For a further discussion of the meaning of *fatara* see Chapter 5. It is sufficient to point out here that this basic disposition with which the humans have been initiated in the creation process is the starting point for all humans on the way of life.)

The upright religion is emphasised in the Qur'an as the total commitment to the way of God using the apparatus provided. This total commitment to the direction of the way of God is called *islam* (3:19). *Islam* is the verbal noun of *aslama*, which means to commit or surrender oneself. In 4:125, the verb *aslama* is used also with *deen* to stress that it is the direction of the way of God that is to be sought and adhere to: who could be on a better course (*deen*) than a person 'who committed (*aslama*) his direction (face)' towards God and does righteous acts?

Origin of the diversity of religions

Starting with this innate tendency of seeking to understand the world they lived in – using the provided apparatus for observation, reasoning and reflection – human beings generated all sorts of views and thoughts concerning the meaning of life and its goal. Although all human efforts in this life commence from the same starting point, the various communities devise ways or views that may be different. These worldviews or ideas will be different in content for all sorts of reasons such as the state of empirical knowledge of the natural surroundings and of human societies at the time and the interplay of all other forces constituting the human personality, especially the socio-political factors. Whenever one proceeds seeking 'the way' in life, the Qur'an says in 16:9, some of the courses that are chosen may be devious. The last part of the verse says that the deviations are essentially the result of the choices made. If humans were not free to choose, which is not the case, all would have automatically been guided.

This intrinsic *deen* or disposition, the basis of our drive to seek or to understand ourselves and the world we live in, is stated again in 42:13 where Muhammad is told that '[God] *started* you on the *road* (started you with the *faith*) ... that was commanded to Noah, Abraham, Moses and Jesus'. Later on in the same unit, Muhammad is told to 'go straight and not to follow the desires of others'. In the above we emphasised *started* and *road* or *faith* because they stand for *shara'a* and *deen*, respectively. The latter was discussed above and represents the intrinsic disposition to seek the truth. The former, *shara'a*, is the verb from which *sharee'ah* is derived and means originally to begin or start on a course. Historically, the course was a watercourse, and this continued to be used until present times. For example, crossing the river Jordan is crossing the *sharee'ah*. The sails of a ship that help to move it on course are called *shiraa's*. However, the use of the verb *shara'a* has been generalised to signify making a course which might be a legislative one for a community, delineating in detail the lines or boundaries which a member of the community may not take or cross. Even the term for a street in a town is called *shaari'*, a derivative of *shara'a*. In the Qur'an, it is used in this general sense to mean a course taken by people. This is explicitly stated also in 5:48, which says that different communities have devised their own courses in life, using the term *shir'ah*, a variation of *sharee'ah*.

The framework of a given worldview (a derived or developed religion with a content) constitutes, or is part of, the faith of the believer in such a system. However, there is an intrinsic faith, whether acknowledged or denied, in all human beings which underlies the phenomenon of learning and seeking the way of the truth. So one may say there is an intrinsic faith in a direction and methodology and a faith in the content of a religion that has been developed along the way of life.

Revelation in the Qur'an

Revelation means a disclosure, an enlightening experience or divine or supernatural communication. Two main words are used in the Qur'an for revelation. The first is *wahy-un* (with *un* for pronunciation only, standing for the nunnation), the verbal noun of the verb *waha* (*wahaya*) meaning 'to reveal', 'inspire' or 'indicate', and some variations of this verb, namely *awha* (the causative form of *waha*) meaning to 'cause inspiration', 'give sign' or 'indicate'. The second usage is based on the verb *nazala*, meaning 'to descend', but mostly in the intensive form (*nazzala*) or the causative form (*anzala*), both with the meaning 'to cause to descend or send down'.

The framework of revelations in the Qur'an are the preachings of Muhammad about the knowledge of the way of God – the One and only one, the Absolute or the solid foundation which cannot be moved (112:2), the Ultimate Truth (31:30), the Sustainer of the World (1:2) – and His plan for the world. Is there a proof for such a God? No, there is no proof; it is a matter of trust or faith and the appealing to one's reason to see that such an overall plan for life and goal meets with the personal satisfaction of the individual, and that it is also good and beneficial for the life of the community. This appeal is also extended to other communities – in the sense that if they wish to continue following their way – to consider working out together a common ground of peaceful coexistence. This is because the Qur'anic revelations predict and recognise that there will always be communities of different faiths, in view of the existence of freedom of choice in the overall plan propounded. This pluralism that is adopted in the Qur'anic discourse does not mean that all the fundamental concepts of the world religions are equally right; the Qur'an is clear about this. The pluralism results from the fundamental principles enunciated in the Qur'an, that humans must choose freely by reasoning and satisfaction and not be forced to believe (see Chapter 5).

This appeal to reason is the main characteristic of the Qur'anic revelations. The revelations emphasise that to gain confidence in that direction, that is, the way of God, one is asked to consider the natural world – the external world outside the human being and the world inside him – wherein are the signs of God. These recommended tools – the observation and examination of the natural world coupled with reasoning and reflection – provide the main arguments for the belief in God and the reasonableness of the overall plan revealed in the Qur'an. This essentially ties the belief in God with mankind's empirical knowledge. This faith in the intelligibility of this world is the basis of all present knowledge. Thus this method of pursuing the signs or indications which would lead towards the knowledge of the way of God is an open-ended avenue of endeavour. The pursuit of the truth is not a short-term project, and will continue until the end of mankind's mandate in this world.

It is clear that the methodology used in the Qur'an to lead humans towards the belief in what the Qur'an calls 'the unseen, the absent from our sights or the unwitnessable world' is not based on speculative philosophy, but on observations of phenomena in our 'witnessable world', the world within and without the human being. The phenomena are available for all to appreciate, consider and reflect upon, although the few who are knowledgeable in the details of such phenomena would be in a more appreciative position (35:28). Knowledge based on observations which is open-ended is more objective than that based on philosophy which tends to be not so open-ended. Philosophy on the whole occupies an intermediate position between science and the arts, as pointed out by Dennett,[9] with the arts being the least objective. These aspects also come into play when considering some modern treatments of religion which abandon objectivity and universality apparently in order to render the contents of such religions immune from criticism.[10]

Revelation as the basis of all knowledge

It is obvious that in the Qur'an, God reveals himself universally in the creation at all times and all places. The revelations tend to tell us that the natural course of evolution of religion progresses with human empirical knowledge. It is clear from the above discussion that religions are a result of human activity and the gained insights or inspirations about the meaning of life result from the use of the endowed apparatus of observation (experience), reasoning and reflection, and thus there is no difference in the mechanism of gaining knowledge in the so-called religious or secular fields. Revelations in both categories are proclaimed in the Qur'an using the same terminology, explicitly stating that they are coming from the same source, namely God. Revelations, in fact, are generalised in the Qur'an, which states that all the knowledge which we attain originates from God (see Chapter 5). Knowledge is achieved, gained or discovered by human beings striving through the learning process, by the act of determining or recognising part of the truth permeating the universe using the apparatus provided.

This process of seeking to understand some aspect of reality by observation and measurement and then arriving at a certain concept is like the meeting of the rays, as it were, of the scanning process of the human mind with part of the reality of the universe, recognising it and then locking on and capturing it so that it becomes part of our accumulated empirical knowledge. Of course one might have a big catch, a small one, a partial catch or an apparent or false catch; it all depends on the individual and his/her capacity.[11] Once we hold onto one end of one thread of the many threads of reality which are interconnected and permeating the universe, eventually we will be led towards the source. This is bearing in mind that according to the Qur'an (24:35), God is the light of the heavens and the earth, and His light permeates the whole universe. This unitary and universal aspect of revelation in the Qur'an becomes clear when it is realised that religion in the singular is only the direction which must be kept in mind when pursuing the various activities of this life (social, political, economical, technical, and so on). These activities cover all sorts of subjects now, which have become differentiated since the Scriptures were written, and no doubt new subjects will be differentiated in the future and old ones will become integrated once more. Learning is at the centre of all the activities of human beings whether in the past, the present or the future, and hence revelations or inspirations inevitably occurred all the time and will continue to occur, generating new knowledge until the end of the mandate of mankind in this world.

What confuses people sometimes when discussing revelation in the Scriptures is the use of the inherited 'religious idiom' where human activities or actions are described in such a way as if they were carried out by God directly with the human person being only a passive receiver or bystander. However, the human being is the seeker in all fields of knowledge, and it is him or her that strives to attain understanding. If some revelations of the Scriptures seem crude, not worthy of being attributed to God, or they are ambiguous, they are so because of their human origin; the inspirations have been affected by human socio-political considerations or by some other human reason.

Before leaving revelation or inspiration, it is of interest to note that the Qur'an uses the same expression, 'God-inspiring', as the driving force for other living beings in their life activities. This is illustrated in 16:68, which says: 'And your Lord revealed unto the bees, saying, take unto yourselves dwellings in mountains and in trees, and in what [men] may build [for you as way of hives].' Clearly, inspirations underlie the natural activities of all living beings. It is also stated that the natural course of the earth and that of the heavens is likewise inspired (see 99:5 and 41:12 respectively). Thus even material systems in the universe evolve in time according to a prescribed or inspired course. It appears, therefore, that there are three levels of consciousness in the creation. The lowest is that of matter, which is the common denominator in the three levels, and has a built-in automatic response to God's command. The next level is generated by a special superstructural arrangement of complex combinations of matter with an intermediate response, as in the example of the bees. The third is characterised by a consciousness with a well-developed voluntary response, as in human beings. These three levels must be related to the intensive swimming or flow (*tasbeeh*) as a response to God's desire.

Revelation in the Bible

In contrast to the above view of revelation, Ward, in a comprehensive study, has recently treated the subject of religion and revelation in which he essentially sees the development of religion as passing through two stages: the primal stage and the world's Canonical Scriptures stage.[12] In the primal stage, humans look at religion as part of the natural world where the progress of religious outlook goes along with the progress of the knowledge of the physical world, both depending on empirical knowledge and experience. Somehow in the transition to the Canonical Scriptures stage a discontinuity seems to be postulated by Ward, where the development of religious revelations becomes separated from the development of knowledge of the physical world with the progression of the latter still dependent on empirical knowledge. However, the knowledge of the Suprasensory Being (God in the theistic religions) is now dependent on revelations where God reveals himself to the various traditions in various and ambiguous ways. This, Ward adds, makes the content of revealed knowledge beyond normal human cognitive capacity as this is not naturally available and must be intentionally communicated.[13] In spite of these statements, it is suggested that revelation occurs in a cooperative fashion[14] and that there is no sharp divide between reason and revelation; for revelation, the active disclosure of spiritual reality, develops precisely as reason.[15] If one takes these two combined mechanisms together with the understanding that Ward is using 'religious idiom', then this may approximate that of the Qur'anic interpretation discussed above, and would make the postulation of two separate mechanisms for the so-called primal and Canonical revelations unnecessary.

What is the nature of revelation in the Bible? Revelation here falls into two kinds, both of which involve God intervening in history in a particular and specific way in order to effect salvation. In the Hebrew Bible, God intervenes directly in history to save the Israelites from the Egyptians and also to conquer Palestine, in order to fulfil the promise revealed earlier to Abraham. Thus in Judaism, divine disclosure is through the control of historical events, as though God were causing water, wind or earth to act in extraordinary or miraculous ways.[16] As this revelation concerns a specific people at a specific time in history and a specific geographical area, it is open to historical investigation. As a result of modern historical investigations, the historicity of the narratives forming the framework of the Hebrew Bible has been put in jeopardy. There is hardly any evidence at all outside the biblical tradition for the stories of the Exodus and for the united monarchies of David and Solomon, not to mention some other parts of the Bible (for more details, see the works of Garbini,[17] Maxwell Miller and Hayes[18] and Redford[19]). Archaeological activities and researches of recent times place most of the historical contents of the Hebrew Bible under a question mark, and writers of history on this subject openly admit that if they were to depend on empirical evidence alone, there would hardly be any history to write about ancient Israel and Judah. Moreover, the narratives which constitute the framework of the Mosaic tradition refer to experiences of other people, the Canaanites, the main antagonists of the Israelites in the Hebrew Bible, as has been stressed by Anderson, who rationalised this process as being similar to new immigrants in America espousing the already established culture. Redford, on the other hand, terms the adoption of the Sojourn and the Exodus themes, which were part of the earlier Canaanite culture, by the Hebrews as ironic.[20]

The Mosaic and the later Prophetic revelations in the Hebrew Bible tend to be mainly tribal and exclusive in nature. Ward points to some moral regression to racist beliefs in these traditions especially when one compares them with those revealed to Abraham.[21] This was also pointed out by Saggs, who quotes a distinguished Jewish scholar saying it was Abraham and not Moses who was the founder of Israel's monotheism.[22] In his comparison of the Islamic and Judaic revelations, Ward suggests that the Islamic revelation universalises the Judaic by rejecting its ethnic basis.

Concerning the New Testament and Christianity, the revelation is also particular in nature and historically based. Here the revelation is based on a particular event where God projected Himself into the realm of human experience in the person of Jesus, appearing as man on earth. Salvation is specified in terms of a number of images and concepts interpreted by reference to the life, death, and resurrection of Jesus. (For a modern discussion of this scheme which occupied Christian thinkers and theologians across the ages, see the several contributions in Gill.[23])

Finally, I would like to end this discussion about revelation by quoting Schleiermacher (as given by Ward): 'What is revelation? Every original and new intuition of the universe is one.'[24]

Part II

THE QUR'AN

3

AN OVERALL VIEW OF THE QUR'AN

Muhammad started his mission when he was forty years old and continued preaching until his death at the age of sixty-three. The inspirations (revelations) which formed Muhammad's preaching discourse over the twenty-three-year period constitute the Qur'an, which means 'the recital' or the proclamation. Muhammad's additional expositions of some aspects of the Qur'anic discourse for various groups, which were collected separately much later under the title of 'Hadeeth', are not treated here. The Qur'an is essentially made up of units arranged in chapters (surahs). A unit may be composed of several sentences. A sentence may be a simple or a very complex one. Some chapters are very short, composed of a single unit; others are very long, made up of many units strung or interwoven together. There are many chapters of intermediate length.

A unit may be a statement, a proclamation, an injunction, a prayer or a preaching unit. A preaching unit may start first by picturing the coming of the Day of Judgement and then the urging that this Day should be taken into consideration during one's lifetime. Man is urged to be grateful to his Lord by doing good works and to avoid the consequences resulting from ignoring this Day. Good works are characterised by being socially relevant, that is, of benefit to society. A preaching unit may also start with an introduction pointing to a phenomenon or phenomena to be considered and reflected upon, ending with the affirmation that for intelligent, thoughtful people, such phenomena are signs pointing towards God. The signs, phenomena or pointers cover all sorts of topics, physical, biological and psychological, which are not necessarily familiar to every person but are dependent on the audience being addressed. Examples include time (several aspects of it, whether to a particular part of the day or to a very long period of

45

time), the sun, the stars, the moon, animals and their uses, trade, wealth, ships, winds, rain, thunder, lightning, plants and the seasons, creation from dust or from water, the formation of life in the womb, the creation of male and female spouses for love and affection, the creation of the heavens and the earth, old age, death, fear, love, aggression, the pen, even the letters of the alphabet and the rise and fall of civilisations.

Each surah stands alone. Since the Qur'an is mainly a preaching discourse occupied to making the human being conscious of God, there is much repetition of preaching units and formulas in the various surahs and even within the same surah. The preaching revolves around a central theme: warning humans that after they die, they will be raised up again and returned to God who will judge them, according to their conduct in this life, at the Day of Reckoning. Therefore they should be conscious of God during this life and follow the direction of the way of God. The way of God is not defined by dogma but is indicated operationally in two ways. The first is practical and socially oriented. It pertains to carrying out actions characterised only by being beneficial to the welfare of humanity (society). The second involves a mental orientation and empirically following a certain procedure. The empirical procedure stresses that the means of gaining faith in God is through observing His creation, thinking (reasoning) and reflecting upon such observations, not in seeking proof but following the direction suggested by such deliberations. Any person who commits or submits (the verb used in Arabic is *aslama*) himself to this course, that is, directs his face (sets his direction) towards God, is a *muslim* (the active participle of *aslama*). Hence we have the word '*islam*' (the verbal noun) describing the religion preached by Muhammad.

The pointers to God are the 'miracles' of God according to Muhammad's inspirations and are the only reliable indicators to Him. From this, one sees they are not miracles in the popular sense of the word. That is, they are not supernatural, but are only manifestations of God's laws as seen in the natural world. Muhammad, during his mission, was pestered and taunted by his opponents to produce a miracle like those reported in the previous Scriptures. His reply to such demands was always that he was only a human being, like everybody else. (It is worth noting here that later Muslims, seeing the extraordinary miracles in the Christian and Jewish Scriptures, invented all sorts of extraordinary happenings and attributed them to Muhammad, all of course outside the Qur'an.)

It is stressed in the Qur'an that all previous messengers and prophets of God were also human. Such statements were directed to Muhammad in order to console and encourage him in the face of the challenges thrown at him to produce something extraordinary. This served as an indirect reply to the question of miracles in the previous Scriptures. There are many verses in the Qur'an directed to Muhammad not only to comfort and console but also to rebuke, for being overzealous or not carrying out his mission properly. This is a reflection of Muhammad's continual interaction with the results and the methods of his preaching and his contemplation upon them, thus resulting in new inspirations.

The Qur'an also contains preachings related to previous prophets. These occur on two levels. One level shows them in the light of Muhammad's mission, as an extension of his message, where the inspirations have been put in the mouths of the ancient prophets or messengers of God. The preaching in this level has several aspects. It encourages Muhammad to pursue his mission by reminding him that the previous prophets faced similar difficulties. It also points to the continuing efforts of humanity to seek the truth and thus to the evolution of the concept of God. The emphasis in this level is on preaching and development of ideas and not history.

The second level deals with the preaching of Muhammad to the Christians and Jews. This preaching involved reminding them of some aspects of their Scriptures or their traditions, the basic deviations from the natural evolutionary course of religion that were introduced, namely the divinity of Jesus and the Judaic exclusiveness (claiming arbitrarily a special position with God exclusively for themselves), and inviting them to the new message which subsumes all what is true in their Scriptures.

Included in the units of the Qur'an are statements and principles that form a plan which establishes the position of man on earth, points to the purpose of life, provides guidance and freedom of choice as well as the necessary tools for the trust or mandate given to mankind. As a consequence of granting freedom of choice to mankind, religious diversity is taken for granted, so the Qur'an contains the principles regulating the dynamic coexistence between the various communities.

The building blocks or units of the Qur'an which have been mentioned or alluded to above cover the major part of the Qur'an, the framework of the Qur'anic discourse. There are other units in the Qur'an which will not be focussed upon in this work. These may be divided into two classes. The first pertains to rituals:

fasting, food restrictions and pilgrimage. These rituals, especially those of the pilgrimage (Hajj), were well established and based on ancient rituals which were part and parcel of the annual festivities in Mecca and its surroundings as well as across the whole of the Arabian Peninsula and its periphery. All that Muhammad has done is to de-paganise these rituals to fit the new outlook. The second category pertains to what may be termed application units, which deal with some aspects of social regulations like inheritance, punishment, marriage and divorce, and so on, which needed immediate attention. These instructions are applications of the principles in the light of customs and circumstances of the local people at the time, and are couched in a preaching manner stressing the observance of the consciousness of God when applying them. To fruitfully discuss them would take us beyond our main objective, since that would entail the enquiry into the prevalent social conditions at that time.

4

A CROSS-SECTION OF THE QUR'AN

Qur'anic units

The inspired revelations to Muhammad have been arranged into 114 surahs. They range in length from the very short, about one line (about 17 words), to the very long, about six hundred lines as they appear now in the standard Arabic text. All the surahs but one begin with the formula 'In the name of God the Compassionate, the Merciful'. This will not be quoted in this work (except for the first surah in which this formula is counted as the first verse), not because it is not important but for clarity's sake (in fact, this formula is used by a Muslim whenever starting any endeavour, whether going to work, beginning a meal, taking a walk or any other action). The arrangement of the surahs in the Qur'an essentially goes from the very long to the very short. The exception is the first chapter, which is a common prayer and is called 'the Opening of the Book'. The numbering (the arrangement of the surahs) is not connected with the sequence of revelation.

In what follows, samples of Qur'anic units will be given dealing with basic aspects of Muhammad's inspirations (revelations). A medium-sized chapter will also be quoted in full (see appendix) to give an idea of a typical structure of a Qur'anic surah. The numbering of the verses in a given surah follows the numbering in the Arabic text. In the translations, however, only the numbers of the first and last verses of the quoted section in a given surah are indicated.

In the text of the translations I have used brackets (...) for alternative meaning or comment. I have also used rectangular brackets [...] to supply the word, phrase or even a clause which is understood or implied in Arabic. Regarding the English translations, I have consulted several translations of the Qur'an.[1] I have also used *A Dictionary and Glossary of the Koran* by John Penrice.[2] I chose what I believed best reflected the meaning of the Arabic text of the Qur'an. Occasionally I have used a word of my own when I felt it gave a better sense.

In what follows, 'God' stands for 'Allaah'. In the Qur'an, the pronunciation of Allaah depends on the grammatical function of the word 'Allaah' in the sentence in question. It is pronounced Allaahu when in the nominative, Allaaha when in the accusative or Allaahi when in the genitive and dative cases, respectively. The word 'Allaah' is an assimilated form of 'Al-ilaah', which, as already discussed, means 'the God'. This assimilation must have started in poetry for ease of flow of sound in reciting. It is common practice in Arabic and biblical Hebrew. 'God' with small g, stands for *ilaah*, the generic name for a deity in Arabic. All the other designations of God in the Qur'an are epithets. An epithet which is used often is *rabb*, which means sustainer, master or head of a family or household, hence translated as lord.

Unit as a statement, a declaration, or an injunction

On God

In the words of Surah 112:

> Say: God is One, the Eternal God. He neither begat nor was begotten. And there is none equivalent to Him.

This proclamation succinctly summarises the concept of God in the Qur'an. There are many verses in the Qur'an which pertain to the concept of God which are dispersed in the various surahs. More samples are given below:

> All that is in the heavens and the earth intensively flows (literally intensively swims) [in gratitude] towards (usually translated extols or praises) God; He is the almighty, the all-wise. It is He that has sovereignty over the heavens and the earth. He ordains life and death, and He has the power to will anything. He is the First and the Last, the Evident [in His creation] and the Hidden [from the human senses];

He has knowledge of everything. It is He that created the heavens and the earth in six days and is established on the seat of power. He knows all that goes in the earth and all that emerges from it, all that comes down from heaven and all that ascends to it. He is with you wherever you may be. God is cognisant of all your actions. He has sovereignty over the heavens and the earth; and unto Him all matters (affairs) are returned.

(Surah 57:1–5)

It is God who has reared the heavens without supports you can see; and is established on the seat of power; and imposed laws on the sun and the moon (made them subservient to His laws): each runs to its appointed term. He directs the Order (Command). He makes His signs (messages) clear, that you may have firm faith in an encounter with your Lord.

(Surah 13:2)

God, there is no god but He, the living, the ever vigilant, slumber seizes Him not, neither sleep. To Him belongs all that is in heavens and the earth. Who is there that shall intercede with Him except by His leave? He knows what lies open before them and what is hidden from them and they do not encompass any of His knowledge save such as He wills. His seat of power comprises the heavens and earth and their upholding does not wary Him. He is the Transcendent, the Great.

(Surah 2:255)

The Qur'an stresses, as will be seen later, that in this world our disputes are to be arbitrated through the use of reason and the sense of justice. The sense of justice is usually derived by an individual or a nation from the concept of God they believe in. The universality of values for all human beings is similarly dependent on the universality of God. A universal and just God will not arbitrarily accept some of his creatures (people) and reject others. It means such a God does everything in the creation according to a standard. This measure or standard is transferred to humans (who believe in such a Deity) to use in their dealings with each other, as individuals or as nations, in this world. Thus the concept of God is the most important part of a theistic religion, especially in the Semitically

51

based Scriptures, and constitutes the general basis of the people's character. This is clear from the following:

> Blessed be He who has sent down upon His servant the standard (the criterion) [by which to discern the true from the false] so that he may be a warner to all beings. His is the dominion over the heavens and the earth; and He has not taken to Him a son, and He has no partner in His dominion. He created everything and determined the measure thereof exactly.
>
> (Surah 25:1–2)

In the following unit, it is stressed that the rewards and punishments God promises to those who believe and carry out righteous works and those who do evil deeds, respectively, will not be fulfilled according to the believer's wishes (i.e. the believers in Muhammad's message) or the wishes of the people of the Book (the Christians and Jews). It will be according to God's promise: whosoever does evil shall be recompensed for it and will not find for him, apart from God, a friend or helper. And whosoever does deeds of righteousness, whether male or female, and he or she a believer (in general which includes believers in God among Christians, Jews, Sabaeans and others as stressed somewhere else in the Qur'an), these shall enter paradise, nor shall they be wronged. This is an important pronouncement which should be taken into consideration whenever prayers are also involved. God is not under the arbitrary command of any human being. As all humans are individually linked to God (see Chapter 5), it is a matter of utilising this linkage that produces the outcome (action). Moreover, belief is something that need not be declared explicitly and publicly since it involves the relationship of the individual with God which is completely a private affair between the individual and God. No other human is privy to it. Only the practical or outward manifestations of the belief of the individual can be witnessed by other human beings. For the indications of what constitute right and evil actions, see, for example, 2:177 or 90:8–18.

> But they who believe and do the things that are right, We will bring them into gardens beneath which the rivers flow; forever shall they abide therein. Truly it is the promise of God: And whose words are more sure than God's? Not according to your wishes, or the wishes of the people

of the Book, shall these things be. He who does evil shall be recompensed for it. Patron or helper, beside God, shall he find none. But whoso does the things that are right, whether male or female, and he/she a believer, these shall enter paradise, nor shall be wronged the skin of a date stone.

(Surah 4:122–124)

In the next statement the universality of direct approach to God is declared. No intermediaries are necessary between humans and God. Muhammad is being told here to proclaim that the lines of communication between God and humans are always open, accessible and at hand. Humans are urged to utilise them directly.

And if My servants (here it signifies all humans including sinners, hence the use of creatures may be better) ask you concerning Me, I am indeed near. I respond to the call of the caller if he calls upon Me. So let them respond to Me and let them believe in Me that they may be guided.

(Surah 2:186)

We return below to the definition of prayers and the implications of calling upon God (13:11), that is, the activation of the bond linking the human to God and not just ordering God as it were to do something or another.

On freedom of religion

The following two samples stress religious freedom and worship. In the second sample it is declared that only God decides at the end, in absolute manner, who was right among the various contestants. God is the only Arbiter in matters of belief. This does not mean ceasing preaching to others. It means all what we can do is to reason with, but not force, others to believe. Belief is founded on conviction.

Say: O unbelievers, I serve (worship) not what you serve and you are not serving what I serve; nor am I serving what you have served, neither are you serving what I serve. You have your religion and I have mine.

(Surah 109)

And thus We revealed it [the Qur'an] in the shape of clear messages and indeed God guides him who wills [to be guided]. Verily, those who believe [in the new message] and those of Jewry, the Sabaeans, the Christians, the Magians and the Idolaters, God will judge between them on the Day of Resurrection. Verily God is witness over everything.

(Surah 22:16–17)

On the creed of Islam

The following declaration gives the best summary of the 'creed' of Islam. It starts by telling us that ritualism is not equal to piety (righteousness). It does not matter to which direction you turn your face in prayer. (Elsewhere in the Qur'an (2:115), we are told whatever direction one turns to in prayers, that would be the direction (face) of God.) It then goes on to define true piety. It covers all aspects of the Qur'anic teachings: the belief in God and the Judgement Day, belief in all the prophets regardless of how ancient they are (thus belief in the human evolutionary concept of God, see later), humility towards God, social obligations towards other human beings, social behaviour in times of adversity, being truthful in dealing with other human beings, and so on.

It is not piety (righteousness) that you turn your faces to the east or west. True piety is this: To believe in God and the last Day, the angels, the Book, and the prophets, to give of one's substance, however cherished, to kinsmen and orphans, the needy, the traveller, and the freeing of human beings in bondage, to perform the prayer, to pay the purification dues (*zakat*).

And they who are true to their promises and steadfast in trial and adversity and time of peril; it is they that have proved themselves true, and it is they who are conscious of God.

(Surah 2:177)

On resurrection time

The Day of Resurrection is one of the pivotal concepts in the preachings of Muhammad and is widely mentioned in the Qur'an. Muhammad was often queried about such a day. The following unit registers the query and the answer to the question. Note also how the course of this life is pictured as that of a ship proceeding to dock at its final destination.

They question you [Muhammad] about the Hour [Resurrection Day], when it shall berth? But how could you tell any thing about it? Only your Lord knows when it will come. Your duty is but to warn those who fear it. It will be on the day when they see it, as if they had tarried but a single evening or at most till the following morn.

(Surah 79:42–46)

On ethics

The following two injunctions directed to the faithful establish a standard of social behaviour and ethics for the new community in dealing with each other and with others outside their community There are no double standards implied here, as can also be seen below in the injunctions concerning the application of justice. The third declaration is directed to all mankind. It establishes the true basis of the coexistence of all peoples on earth. The position of honour in the sight of God is open to all. There are no specially favoured people who are arbitrarily chosen.

O you who believe: let not any people scoff at another people; it may well be that those [whom they deride] are better than themselves. And no women [shall deride other] women; it may well be that those [whom they deride] are better than themselves. And find not fault with one another, neither revile one another with nicknames. An evil name, is ungodliness after attaining faith.

O you who believe: eschew much suspicion, for some suspicion is a sin. And do not spy, neither backbite one another; would any of you like to eat the flesh of his dead brother? No, you would loathe it. And be conscious of God; assuredly God is an acceptor of repentance, merciful.

O mankind, We have created you from a male and a female, and have made you into nations and tribes, that you may know one another. Verily the noblest among you in the sight of God is the one who is most conscious of Him. God is all-knowing, all-aware.

(Surah 49:11–13)

On justice

In the next two injunctions, the standard of justice is established.

> O believers, be you securers of justice, witnesses for God. And let not detestation for a people move you not to be equitable; be equitable – that is nearer to the consciousness of God. So be conscious of God; verily, God is aware of all that you do.
>
> (Surah 5:8)

> O you who believe: be securers of justice, witnesses for God, even though it be against yourselves, or your parents and kinsmen, whether the party be rich or poor. God is nearer than you to both. Therefore do not follow the desires lest you swerve from truth. And if you distort or decline [your testimony], know that God is cognisant of all your actions.
>
> (Surah 4:135)

On self-defence

The following injunction establishes the principle of self-defence.

> And fight in the way of God with those who fight with you, but do not commit aggression: verily, God does not love the aggressors.
>
> (Surah 2:190)

The statements one finds in the Qur'an regarding fighting are neither pacifist nor aggressive, but are defensive and reciprocal. Because of the widespread accusation or belief that the religion of Islam was spread by the 'sword', it may be of interest to digress a little and point out here that unlike the Bible, the word 'sword' is not mentioned in the Qur'an at all. It is, however, widely mentioned in the Hebrew Bible. This is probably to be expected as a reflection of tribal warfare and the involvement of tribal gods (the God of Israel versus the gods of the Canaanites, and so on), as for example in Deuteronomy 20:13. Of more interest, however, is the reported declaration attributed to Jesus (Matthew 10:34): 'You must not think that I have come to bring peace on the earth; I have not come to bring peace, but a sword.'

On man–woman relationships and the basis of marriage

And of His signs is that He created for you, of yourselves, spouses, that you may repose in them, and has put love (affection) and tenderness (mercy) between you. Herein truly are signs for those who reflect.

(Surah 30:21)

Here both males and females are addressed, as is clear from the use of the word spouses which is in Arabic *azwaj*, the plural of *zawj* which literally means 'pair', signifying either a husband or a wife.

Unit as a prayer

Prayers are acts of worship. They may be looked upon as the psychological preparations preceding human actions or endeavours in anticipation for dealing with them, or they may be confessions of guilt or sin. They represent an attempt on the part of humans to communicate with God for guidance, help or protection from some danger; or to ask forgiveness for mistakes or bad deeds committed and also to render thanks. In any case, requests from God for help are bound by many limitations such as 4:122–124 quoted above, which warns us that God deals equitably with all human beings according to fixed principles and not according to our wishes and whims.

Prayers in the Qur'an fall into two categories, *salaat* and *du'aa'* (supplication). *Salaat*, which may be termed the canonical or official prayer, has a standard form and appears to be partly ritualistic in the sense of drills or exercising in sports or the army. *Du'aa'*, which is private in nature, has no official standard form. Prayers, *salaat* and *du'aa'*, being attempts of communication with God, constitute an important part of the preachings of Muhammad. The subject of *salaat* has recently been treated in detail by Monnott, who sketched all aspects of its development and evolution in the Qur'an as well as its central importance.[3]

What is the standard form of *salaat*? *Salaat* is composed of a minimum of two and a maximum of four prayer units. A prayer unit consists of presenting oneself before God standing on a clean spot reciting the official prayer, which is the first surah of the Qur'an, also called 'the Opening of the Book'. Other verses from the Qur'an may also be recited in addition to the first surah. The recitation is followed by bowing and prostration, during both of which obedience of the Almighty is proclaimed. A full prayer (*salaat*) is made of a minimum of two or a maximum of four of these units, depending on the time of the day. At the end of prayer one enters again in life activity by declaring '*assalum alaykum*', in the right and left directions, as if one was returning from a trip.

The *salaat* is carried out by individuals singly or in groups (in the latter case, one of the group leads the prayer) and is meant to instil in the believer the discipline of remembering God during the day (waking hours).

Surah 1 (the Opening of the Book):

> In the name of God the Merciful, the Compassionate. Praise belongs to God, Lord of the Universe, the Compassionate, the Merciful, Sovereign of the Day of Judgement. You alone we worship, and You alone we turn for help. Guide us to the straight path, the path of those whom You have favoured, not of those against whom You are wrathful, nor of those who have gone astray.

The performance of prayers is preceded by the ritual of purification (washing). These acts are not all delineated in the Qur'an.

Although there is no standard form for *du'aa'* some general forms are found in the Qur'an. Two samples are given below.

> God does not charge a person with more than one's capacity. In his favour shall be whatever good he does, and against him whatever evil he does. O Our Lord (Rabbana), take us not to task if we forget or unwittingly do wrong. O Our Lord, lay not upon us a burden such as You did lay upon those who lived before us. O Our Lord, do not charge us with more than we can bear, and pardon us and forgive us and have mercy upon us. You are our Master, and help us against the people who are ungrateful (the rejecters of Your signs or messages).
>
> (Surah 2: 286)

> Say: I seek refuge with the Lord of mankind, the Sovereign of mankind, the God of mankind, from the evil of the silent whisperer, who whispers in the hearts of mankind (people in general, familiar and unfamiliar human beings), from the *jinn* (i.e. unfamiliar human beings) and *al-naas* (the familiar human beings).
>
> (Surah 114)

See Chapter 5 for a further discussion on *jinn*.

Preaching units

Essentially the whole discourse of the Qur'an revolves around preaching, and this can be seen in all sections of the Qur'an. Therefore only few representative samples will be given here. In the following two units, the preaching is introduced by portraying signs of the coming of the Day of Judgement. On that day, humans will be presented with the records of their actions in their lifetimes in this world, on the basis of which they will be judged and rewarded or punished.

> When the earth quakes with her [last] quaking, and [when] the earth yields up her burdens, and the human cries out: what has happened to her? On that Day she will recount her tidings, as your Lord will have inspired her to do. On that Day all people will come forward, separated (dispersed), to be shown their [past] deeds. And so, he who does an atom's weight of good, shall see it; and he who does an atom's weight of evil shall see it.
>
> (Surah 99)

An atom means here the smallest particle which is visible to the naked eye. It could also be the smallest ant. The point here is that regardless of how small the action is, it will be recorded.

> When the sky is rent asunder; when the stars scatter and the seas burst beyond their bounds; and when the graves are overturned, every person shall know what he has done and what he failed to do. O human being! what is it that lures you away from your bountiful Lord; who created you, gave you an upright form, and proportioned you? In whatever shape which pleased Him has He fashioned you. Even so; but you treat the Last Judgement as a lie. Yet truly there are guardians over you – illustrious recorders – cognisant of all your actions. The righteous will surely dwell in bliss. But the wicked shall burn in Hell upon the Judgement Day, nor shall they escape from it. But do you conceive what the Judgement Day will be? And once again, do you conceive what that Day will be? [It will be] a Day

when no person shall be of the least avail to another person: for on that Day all sovereignty is God's alone.

(Surah 82)

The following preaching unit is introduced by drawing of a moving picture of the onset of a violent raiding scene. This is then followed by a sudden turn stressing man's ingratitude to his God, his great capacity for greed and his intense love of good things. Then the human being is reminded of the Day of Judgement, when everything will be unfolded as God is well informed of all.

By the snorting chargers (i.e. horses), by the strikers of fire (as a result of the hoofs hitting the ground), by the dawn raiders, blazing a trail of dust, cleaving there with a host, verily man is ungrateful to his Lord; and surely he is a witness against that; and truly he is passionate in his love for good things. Ah! does he not know that when the dead are thrown out from their graves and men's hidden thoughts are laid open, their Lord will on that day have full knowledge of them all.

(Surah 100)

In the next unit, the phenomenon alluded to is 'time'.

By the flight of time, verily the human being is bound to lose himself unless he be of those who have faith and do righteous deeds and council each other unto the truth and council each other to be steadfast.

(Surah 103)

The next illustration of preaching is more complex. It points to more than one phenomenon (sign of God) to be considered. It starts by pointing to the daybreak phenomenon, then the first ten days of the month, which the people of Mecca considered sacred. This is then followed by pointing to the even and odd numbers and to the night that runs its course (that is, moving on and disappearing). The next phenomenon noted is the rise and fall of certain civilisations, the remains of which were known to Muhammad's audience. Then the preaching follows, reminding the audience of how man behaves in difficult and easy times as well as of some socially undesirable practices in which they are engaged. It ends as usual with reminding them of the coming of the Day of Judgement and the consequences of the actions taken in one's lifetime.

By the dawn and the ten nights, by the even [number] and the odd, by the night when it journeys on! Is there not in that an oath for a mindful person? Have you not seen what your Lord did with 'Aad, [the people of] Iram of the pillars, the like of which was never created in the land; and Thamood who hollowed the rocks in the valley, and Pharaoh of the [many] tent-poles, who all transgressed in the land and multiplied corruption therein? Therefore your Lord poured on them a scourge of chastisement. Verily your Lord is ever on the watch. As for the human being whenever his Lord tries him, and honours him, and blesses him, then he says: my Lord has honoured me. But when he tries him, and stints for him his provisions, then he says: my Lord has despised me. But no, no, you do not honour the orphan, nor urge one another to feed the needy, and you devour the inheritance [of others] with devouring greed and you love wealth with exceeding love. No indeed; [how will you fare on Judgement Day] when the earth is crushed and [the Majesty of] your Lord stands revealed, as well as [the true nature of] the angels, rank upon rank? And that Day, hell will be brought [within sight]; upon that day the human being will remember [all that he did and failed to do]: but will that remembrance avail him? He will say: Oh, would that I had forwarded for my life [to come].

Upon that day none shall chastise as He chastises, and none shall bind as He binds. [To the righteous, God will say]: O human being at peace with your self, return to your Lord, well-pleased, well-pleasing, and enter among My servants and enter My Paradise.

(Surah 89)

A medium-sized surah (Surah 30) is presented in the appendix as a further illustration of the structure of a typical Qur'anic surah and the complex interwoven preaching units showing some of the repetitive aspect of preaching formulas. This is one of 29 surahs in the Qur'an which start with single letters of the alphabet, standing singly and not forming a word. In this surah, these letters are 'A', 'L' and 'M'. This phenomenon must be treated as an abstract form of a sign of God, pointing to the learning process of writing and reading which is a characteristic human activity. It is worth mentioning here that the first inspired part of the Qur'an was Surah 96:1–5: 'Recite in the name of your Lord ... who taught by the pen, [He] taught the human that he knew not.'

Another surah of the Qur'an (Surah 68) starts by a single letter 'N', which is followed immediately by: 'By the pen and what they inscribe.' This again signifies learning. All the other surahs starting with symbolic letters point explicitly to the Book, the Qur'an.

After the single letters, a political event is mentioned in what appears to be a prediction. However, this should not be treated as such, because this would go against the spirit of Muhammad's mission and all that the Qur'an stands for. The Qur'an does not deal with the predictions of such happenings. It is explicitly stated in more than one place in the Qur'an that Muhammad is a mortal, like anyone else, that it was indicated (revealed) to him that God is One God (18:110) and that he was only a warner and not able to foresee the future (6:50).

In Surah 6:50, Muhammad is instructed to say also that he only followed what was revealed (indicated by inspiration) to him. This refers to his main mission, mentioned in many places in the Qur'an and exemplified by Surah 18:110 (quoted later in full), about the preaching of the oneness of God and the direction leading to the way of God. Muhammad's position regarding the knowledge of the unwitnessable events in this world (unwitnessable because they have not yet occurred) is represented by Surah 7:188, which instructs him to:

> Say: I have not the power to acquire benefits for – or to avert evil (hurt) from – myself, except as God wills. Had I knowledge of the unknown (the unseen, the future) I would have availed myself of much that is good and no harm would have touched me. But I am only a warner and an announcer of good news to a people believing firmly.

The idiom 'as God wills', concerning human actions and inspiration more generally, is discussed below. Therefore, the verse should be read as a hope for this event to happen in the future. This is then followed by stressing that the Order (Command) of this universe is God's, in the past and in the future. On that (hopeful) day, the believers shall rejoice in God's help who gives help to whom He wills. That is God's promise. Some preaching follows, reminding the audience (or readers) amongst other things that God has created the heavens and the earth and all that is between them with the truth and for a stated term. They are told that the demise of earlier civilisations was a result of their actions and not due to God's injustice. This is followed by stressing that mankind will be returned to God and believers in, and deniers of, the truth will be judged and receive their respective dues.

A series of 'signs' of God are then marshalled as pointers towards God which should be considered and reflected upon. This is followed by preaching, emphasising again that God, who created man in the first instance, will bring him to life again after his death. Then we meet verses addressed to Muhammad personally concerning the difficulties he was facing in discharging his mission. These will be discussed separately below. Muhammad is told to set his direction (face) inclining to the religion (way), that is, God's original creation upon which He disposed mankind, and not to be unsettled.

We see in this surah, as in Surah 89 already quoted, that righteous work is associated with expending some of what one cherishes on various categories of causes, and that denial of the truth is connected with following one's excessive selfish desires or lust. We also meet an urging to avoid usury and are told that it is better in the sight of God to give *zakat*, the wealth purification dues.

Units concerning Muhammad's discharge of his mission

These units abound in the Qur'an. All stress his humanity in order to dispel the idea widespread at the time that a messenger of God is equipped for his mission with supernatural powers. They tell us that Muhammad was a normal human being subject to doubt, depression, anxiety, favouritism, impatience and overeagerness in pursuing his mission. The units fall into several categories: consoling, encouraging, rebuking and correcting. It must be kept in mind that the rest of the Qur'anic discourse falls largely under the categories of preaching or instructing. The samples below illustrate the above points.

By the forenoon and the brooding night, your Lord has not forsaken you, nor does He scorn you, and the Last shall be better for you than the First. And indeed your Lord shall give you, and you shall be satisfied. Did He not find you an orphan, and shelter you? and found you lost [in your way], and guided you? Did He not find you needy and suffice you? Therefore do not oppress (break the spirit of) the orphan, nor scold that seeks [your] help; and declare your Lord's blessings and favours.

(Surah 93)

Did We not expand your heart (the opposite of depression) and relieve you of the burden which weighed down your back? Did We not raise you high in dignity? So truly, with hardship comes ease, truly with hardship comes ease. So when you are freed [of your distress] resume your task and seek your Lord with fervour.

(Surah 94)

He [Muhammad] frowned and turned away when the blind man came to him. How could you [Muhammad] tell that he (the blind man) would not get purification [of self] [by deciding to turn your back on him]? He might have received an admonition which would have benefited him. But to the wealthy man you were all attention; although the fault would not be yours if he remained unpurified. Yet to him that came to you eagerly and with awe [of God], you gave no heed.

(Surah 80:1–10)

The above rebuking is followed by general preaching stressing that the mission of Muhammad is a reminder (a warning) directed to all who are willing. In the next unit, Muhammad's humanity is emphasised by the declaration that he possesses no supernatural powers. Again he is warned not to reject those who are keen on the new message, regardless of their social standing.

[Muhammad,] say: I do not tell you that I possess God's treasures, or know what is not witnessable, nor do I claim to be an angel. I follow only that which is revealed to me. Say: are the blind and the seeing man equal? Will you not reflect?

And warn hereby those who fear lest they be gathered unto their Lord with none to protect them from Him or to intercede with Him, so that they might become conscious of Him. Hence repulse not [any of] those who, at morn and evening, invoke their Lord, seeking His Countenance. Nothing of their account falls upon you, and nothing of your account falls upon them, that you should drive them away, and so become one of the evildoers.

(Surah 6:50–52)

This theme is stressed again in the next passage, telling Muhammad that he is only a warner with no power to force people to believe. The reckoning belongs to God and not to Muhammad.

Therefore remind them; you are only a reminder. You have no power over them. As for those who turn their backs and disbelieve, God will inflict on them the supreme chastisement. To Us they shall return, and upon Us shall rest their reckoning.

(Surah 88:21–26)

In the next unit, we see the pressure exerted on Muhammad as a result of the challenges thrown upon him by his opponents, which were beginning to affect him so that he started thinking of diluting his message in order to accommodate them. Again he is told he is only a warner, and to stick to his mission.

Perchance you may be inclined to give up a part of what is revealed to you because you are distressed by their saying: why has a treasure not been sent down to him, or an angel not come with him? But you are only a warner. God is a guardian over everything. Or when they say: he forged it (the Qur'an). Say to them: produce ten forged surahs like it; and call upon whom you are able, apart from God, if you speak truly. But if they fail you, know that it is revealed with God's knowledge, and that there is no God but He, so are you submitting [yourselves unto Him]?

(Surah 11:12–14)

In the next unit we see that the pressure on Muhammad has increased so much that he is tempted to substitute some of his earlier inspirations with something else in order to accommodate his opponents. Muhammad is warned about this, and is reminded of the consequences which would follow if he takes that course.

Indeed they were at the point of tempting you
[Muhammad] away from that which We revealed to you,
with a view to making you substitute in Our name something quite different, in which case they would have taken
you as a friend. Indeed had We not made you stand firm
[in faith] you might have inclined to them a little. In that
case We would have made you taste double [chastisement]
in life and double [chastisement] after death and you would
have found none to help you against Us.

(Surah 17:73–77)

The same theme is pursued in the next unit.

Those to whom the Scriptures were given, rejoice in what
is revealed to you [Muhammad], but some factions deny a
part of it. Say: I am commanded to serve God and to associate none with Him; to Him I call, and to Him I shall return. Thus, then, We have sent the Qur'an as a code
(ordinance) in the Arabic tongue; and truly, if after the
knowledge that has reached you [Muhammad], you follow
their desires, you shall have no guardian against God.

(Surah 13:36–37)

In the next quotation, the position and mission of Muhammad
are put succinctly.

[Muhammad,] say: I am only human, the like of you; it is
revealed to me that your God is but One God. Hence,
whoever looks forward for the encounter with his Lord let
him do righteous deeds and not associate with his Lord's
service anyone.

(Surah 18:110)

The righteous deeds recommended to bring humans nearer to God,
as we have noted in Surah 2:177 and repeatedly mentioned in the
Qur'anic discourse, all relate to the removal of injustices in society.

Units stressing that all messengers of God are mortal

This is a continuation of the previous topic. The emphasis of this
aspect is very important because it gives indirect answers to

questions which have been raised concerning the ability of the messengers of God to perform supernatural actions (the so-called miracles). Muhammad was taunted and challenged to prove that he was a messenger of God by producing miracles like those reported in the Bible. His reply was that he was only a human being like everybody else, and a warner. He did not go around saying that all the reported miracles were nonsense or they were exaggerated stories about the messengers of God. Instead, he concentrated on the humanity of the messengers of God and their inspiration by God. Later we will see that God does not directly interfere in human affairs by carrying out supernatural things, either for attracting the attention of people or for repelling dangers from people regardless of how evil humans could be to each other. The only signs which point towards God in this world, according to the Qur'an, are in nature: the total creation.

Mankind has been put on trial and entrusted with full responsibility to run its affairs in this life, and it is up to people to do the right things and fight evil in light of their belief in God. This again points to the importance of adopting a concept of God that is universal with respect to all mankind, as it is from God we derive our sense of justice. This is of the utmost importance for peace in this world. Regarding God's will in human affairs and inspiration, they are idioms which were (and are) part of inherited religious discourse and relate to human deliberations and the choices they freely make (see below). The following samples should be sufficient to illustrate the point under consideration.

> Nor were the messengers whom We sent before you [Muhammad] other than men inspired by Our Will and chosen from among their people.
>
> (Surah 12:109)

> We have sent forth other messengers before you [Muhammad] and gave them wives and offspring; and it was not for any messenger to bring a message, but by God's will.
>
> (Surah 13:38)

> The messengers We sent before you [Muhammad] were but men, whom We inspired. Ask the people of the Remembrance, if you do not know. Nor did We fashion them as bodies that ate no food, neither were they immortals.
>
> (Surah 21:7–8)

Never did We send a messenger or a prophet before you [Muhammad] but, when he framed a desire, Satan threw some [vanity, fancy] into his desire. But God abrogates (erases) what Satan casts and then makes precise His messages. Surely God is all-Knowing Wise.

(Surah 22:52)

It is abundantly clear that the messengers of God were humans who were inspired but who could also, like other humans, be tempted by Satan and fall prey to their own wishful thinking. We meet in the above quotation the term 'God abrogates'. This is related to the subject of inspiration and evolution of religion. It is to be noted here that the abrogation mentioned above occurs within the lifetime of one person.

Units relating preachings and legends of previous prophets

These occur on two levels. On the first level, the preachings related are a reflection of Muhammad's mission; they stress his general preaching and the arguments raised against his mission, and not the history of the prophets in whose mouths the words were put. They stress the continuity of preaching the worship of the One God as revealed to Muhammad. It is emphasised that all the preachings of all messengers of God (the Qur'an pictures them as a single community seeking God, Surah 23:51–52) have a unitary aim across the ages, which is the seeking of the ultimate reality, God.

Although there is a single aim which is stressed, it is inevitable that there would be different models adopted at various times. These models or mental pictures which have been adopted across the ages depend on the experiences and the understandings of creation by humanity at those particular times, and of which God is aware (23:51). The different models are not expounded or detailed in the Qur'an (except for a brief mention in 6:75–79, as discussed below) but they are mentioned by the general term 'Book'. This is the standard form in which these preachings appeared by the time of Muhammad. The process of inspiration and the adoption of new mental pictures or models at various times has been generalised in the Qur'an. In Surah 13:38, it is explicitly stated that: 'to every age its Book'. Thus these different experiences and insights leading to different models are taken as natural in the Qur'an.

This natural evolution in outlook is also implied by the many statements (for example, in 2:124–141 below) which declare the necessity of belief in all previous messengers of God regardless of how ancient they were. This belief is part of the creed of Islam. The implications are quite clear for the evolutionary development of models in religion. The belief in all the prophets and messengers of God is essential in order to stress the continuity of the human effort seeking the ultimate reality. The proclamation (13:38) that each age has its own book (inspiration) is the practical manifestation of this effort. By necessity, there would be changes in outlook from one age to another. This is indicated in Surah 13:39, immediately following 13:38, which declares: 'God abrogates (erases, annuls) and confirms (establishes) whatever He wills [of His earlier messages] – for with Him is the source of inspiration (the mother of the Book).'

What God 'does or wills' in human affairs (in other words, God 'abrogating' or 'establishing', as noted above), is a religious idiom signifying what humans themselves choose to do, whether discarding old ideas (abrogating) or keeping others (confirming), as discussed further in Chapter 5. This means that the changes occur naturally in accordance with the changes in the experience of mankind resulting from empirical observations, reasoning and reflection. This, of course, may occur within one lifetime, as pointed out above.

It is worth noting that the symbolic Adam, representing the beginning of humanity and the start of consciousness and of the voluntary seeking of God (because there is a choice available), is taken as the first of the prophets or messengers of God (3:33). This tells us that the election or choice to carry out God's messages, to put it in religious idiom, or the ability to be inspired and preach the resulting inspiration if put in naturalistic language, is open to any human being. It is worth digressing a little to point to what I call the 'politics of preaching' in 3:33–34. (It is to be noted that the statement is phrased in such a way as if it is agreeing with the audience's belief about a certain election, of the family of Abraham or of the family of Amram, the father of Moses and Haroun: but in the same statement the election is generalised to the whole human race through the election of Noah and above all of Adam, the symbol for mankind.)

We should also point out the explicit mention in the Qur'an of the evolutionary concept of the deity (in Surah 6:75–79, quoted and discussed below) which is based on observation, reasoning and reflection. Thus we see in the Qur'an two aspects to the seeking of the way of God. The first concerns human conception, which depends on our accumulated empirical knowledge, and which the Qur'an tells us to be natural, since all our experiences are empirically based and learning is a continuous process. As we gain in experience and realise our misconceptions, the old concepts are naturally discarded in time or, using the Qur'anic 'religious idiom', they are abrogated (erased). The second aspect, which is not connected with the human conception of reality, pertains to the real workings of God's creation: the totality of the laws of nature, God's original enactment. This is unchangeable. The pursuit of this order is our only reliable indicator to the way of God.

The first level: an extension of Muhammad's message

And We sent Noah to his people; and he said: O my people, serve God, you have no God other than He. Will you not be conscience of Him. The council of unbelievers among his people said: This is naught but a mortal like yourselves, who desires to gain superiority over you. And if God willed, He would have sent down angels. We never heard of this among our fathers, the ancients. He is naught but a man bedevilled; so wait on him for a time. He said: O my Lord, help me, for that they cry me lies. Then We said to him: Build an ark under Our watchful eyes and according to Our instructions. When Our judgement comes to pass and water wells out from the oven, take aboard a pair from every species and the members of your household, except those of them already doomed. Do not plead with me for those who have done wrong: they shall be drowned. And when you and all your followers have gone aboard, say: Praise be to God who has delivered us from the people of the evildoers.

(Surah 23:23–28)

In the above unit we have essentially two parts. The first part covers the preaching for the worship of the One God, as indicated to Muhammad but put in the mouth of Noah. The preaching discourse and the reaction to it reflect Muhammad's situation. The second part reverts to Noah's situation very briefly in a most general way for the benefit of those who heard the biblical story in order to stress principles arising from Muhammad's preaching. There is no history involved.

> And after those [people of old] We gave rise to new generations and We sent unto them a messenger from among themselves, and he said: O my people, serve God, you have no God other than He. Will you not, then, take heed? But the unbelieving elders of his people, who denied the encounter of the life to come, and on whom We had bestowed the good things of this life, said: This man is but a mortal like yourselves, who eats of what you eat and drinks of what you drink. If you obey a mortal like yourselves, then you will be losers.
>
> What! does he threaten you that when you are dead and become dust and bones, you shall be brought forth? Far-fetched, far-fetched indeed, is what you are promised. There is nothing but our present life; we die and we live, and we shall not be raised from the dead. He is nothing but a man who forged lies against God, and we are not going to believe him. He [the messenger] said: O my Lord, help me against their accusation of lying. He replied: Before long they will be remorseful. The Cry seized them justly, and We swept them away like withered leaves; and so, away with evildoing folk.
>
> (Surah 23:31–41)

The above unit tells us that generations later, another messenger of God was sent to preach to his people the worship of the One God. It also talks about the arguments raised against such preachings. Again we see that the preaching as well as the arguments raised against it are a replica of Muhammad's situation, except for the specific end result for the deniers of the truth. This general picture is stressed again in the following unit, which tells us that as time passed other messengers of God were sent, one after another including Moses and Jesus, to preach the worship of God. The unit ends with the declaration that all the preachings of all messengers of God are known to God and that all of these messengers form a single community seeking God.

> Then We raised after them other generations, [for] no community can ever forestall [the end of] its term and neither can they delay [its coming]. And We sent forth Our

messengers, one after another; and every time there came to a community its messenger, they accused of lying, and so We caused them to follow one another [in the grave], and let them become [mere] tales; and so – away with the folk who would not believe.

And We sent Moses and his brother Aaron with Our signs and with clear authority unto Pharaoh and his great ones; but these behaved with arrogance, and they were a lofty people. And they said: What! shall we believe two mortals like ourselves, whose people are our servants? So they cried them lies, and they were among the destroyed.

And We gave Moses the Book, so that they might find the right way. And We made the son of Mary and his mother a sign, and provided for both an abode in a lofty place of lasting restfulness and unsullied springs.

O Messengers, eat of the good things and do righteous deeds: verily, I have full knowledge of all what you do. And verily, this community of yours is one single community, since I am the Lord of you all; remain, then, conscious of Me.

(Surah 23:42–52)

In the following unit the evolutionary concept of the perception of God by human beings and its dependence on empirical observations, reasoning and reflection is explicitly stated. It is put in the mouth of Abraham. This discourse, however, is not to be found in the Hebrew Bible (see Genesis 15:5) nor the midrashic commentaries on Genesis.[4] This methodology is the most characteristic of Muhammad's mission, which used preaching in order to indicate the way to gain faith in God. It does not involve drawing on the 'tradition' of his audience in order to remind them of their beliefs, as happens in the second level of Muhammad's preachings to the people of the Book (see below). This methodology or way to gain faith pervades the Qur'anic discourse. It is described in the following unit as Abraham's creed.

And thus We gave Abraham insight into God's mighty dominion over the heavens and the earth, that he might be of those having sure faith. Then when the night overshadowed him with its darkness he saw a star, he said: that is my Lord; but when it set he said: I love not [gods] which set. And then when he saw the moon rising, he said: this is my Lord; but when it set, he said: surely if my God does not guide me, I shall be of the people gone astray.

Then when he saw the sun rising, he said: this is my Lord, this is greater. But when it [too] went down he said: O my people, I am free of [the abomination] of what you associate [with God]. I have turned my face to Him who originated the heavens and the earth, a man of pure faith; and I am not one of the idolaters.

(Surah 6:75–79)

The following is another example of Muhammad's preachings which stresses the continuity and evolution of religious concepts. It also touches on the preaching to the people of the Book, but with limited retelling from the Bible. The unit (2: 130–141), following earlier verses describing Abraham and his son Ishmael's establishment of the Temple at Mecca, declares that only a foolish person would turn away from the creed of Abraham (concerning the use of observation, reasoning and reflection in the process of seeking God). Then it is stressed that Abraham, Ishmael, Isaac, Jacob and the grandchildren (the Tribes) were not Jews (that is, not followers of Judaism) or Christians, but natural worshippers of God at their time. (The natural disposition of seeking God in accordance with one's empirical experience is stressed in the Qur'an and has been alluded to earlier in Surah 30:30.) Then it is declared that those people (Abraham, Isaac, and so on) have passed away: 'They shall receive what they had earned, and you (the Children of Israel) shall receive what you earn.' This formula is mentioned more than once, emphasising that each people are responsible for their actions only and therefore it is best to concentrate on the present and stop arguing about past generations.

Finally, to the saying that only Christians or Jews would be guided, Muhammad is told to say that he follows the creed of Abraham. This means the natural progressive evolutionary course based on observations (experience) and the use of reasoning and reflection in seeking the way of God or the truth. Following this course necessitates the acknowledgement of all the messengers of God from the earliest times up to the present time, making no distinction between them. This is because no religious concept is born in a vacuum. As was stressed in the introduction to this section, all messengers of God have the same aim – the seeking of the ultimate reality – but their experiences, inevitably, are different. Each time has its own model, mental picture or book.

The choice or election which is stressed below is that of the methodology established to gain faith — empirical observations, reasoning and contemplation, as discussed above — and not genealogical, as is clear from the context. A sweeping genealogical choice or exaltation is categorically ruled out in Surah 2:124. This methodology or way to gain faith, which is at the centre of Muhammad's inspirations and is called the creed of Abraham, is open to all humans, as was indicated above concerning Surah 3:33–34.

And who, unless he be weak of mind, would abandon Abraham's creed? We chose him in this world, and in the world to come he shall be among the righteous. When His Lord said to him: submit [your face, direction,] he said: I have submitted [my face, direction] unto (towards) the Lord of all the worlds. And Abraham enjoined this creed on his sons, and [so did] Jacob: My sons, God has chosen for you the religion (the way), so do not allow death to overtake you before you have submitted [your direction] unto (towards) Him.

And you yourselves [children of Israel] bear witness that when death was approaching Jacob, he said unto his sons: Whom will you worship when I am gone? They answered: We will worship your God, the God of your fathers Abraham and Ishmael and Isaac, One God; and unto Him we will submit [our faces, direction].

Now those people have passed away; unto them shall be accounted what they have earned, and unto you, what you have earned; and you will not be questioned about their actions.

And they say: Be Jews or Christians and you shall be guided. Say: Nay, but [ours is] the creed of Abraham, who turned away from all that is false, and was not of those who associate other divinities with God.

[Muhammad,] Say: We believe in God, and in that which was sent down on us and sent down on Abraham, Ishmael, Isaac and Jacob, and their children (i.e. the Tribes), and that which was given to Moses and Jesus and the Prophets, by their Lord; we make no distinction between any of them, and unto Him we submit [our faces, direction].

And if they believe in the like of that you [Muhammad] believe in, then they are truly guided; but if they turn away, then they are clearly separating themselves from you, and God will suffice you for them; He is the All-hearing, the All-knowing. [Say: Our life takes its] hue from God; and who could give a better hue [to life] than God? and Him do We serve.

Say [Muhammad,] [to the Jews and Christians]: Do you argue with us about God, who is our Lord and your Lord? Our deeds belong to us, and to you belong your deeds; Him we serve sincerely. Or, do you claim that Abraham and Ishmael and Isaac and Jacob and the Tribes were 'Jews' or 'Christians'? Say [Muhammad,]: Who knows best, you, or God? And who could be more wicked than he who suppresses a testimony given to him by God? Yet God is not unmindful of what you do.

Now those people have passed away; they have the reward of their deeds, and for you is the reward of yours; but of their doings you shall not be questioned.

(Surah 2:130–141)

The second level: preaching to the people of the Book

The second level in relating stories and legends of previous prophets shows the preaching of Muhammad to the Christian and Jewish communities. It is a continuation of the above preaching, but there is much retelling from the 'traditions' of these communities. It is important to stress this, especially for readers who are not familiar with the details of the biblical text. Muhammad was very keen on winning over both communities to the new way, striving to accommodate them without compromising the basic message of his mission. As can be seen from the many units in the Qur'an on this subject, much material from the Hebrew Bible has been retold when preaching to the Jewish community: while simultaneously indicating deviations from the natural course of religious evolution they introduced and then inviting listeners to the new message. Similarly, Christians are addressed in passages which stress the denial of the divinity of Jesus.

In the following first section (2:40–54), which is a small part of a large section in Surah 2 of the Qur'an dealing with this topic, the 'Children of Israel' are alternately being reminded on the one hand of all the favours God bestowed on them at the time of Moses and

on the other of their deviations, disobedience and rebellions at that
time. In both of these instances, the praising and the rebuking are
done in accordance with the Torah and other books of the Hebrew
Bible, such as Exodus 32, Jeremiah 7, Nehemiah 9, and so on.

These two aspects, the bestowing of the favours of God on, and
the extreme anger of God with, the Children of Israel, which one
finds in the following verses, are not Muhammad's invention but
are in accordance with what is in the Hebrew Bible. These two
aspects, the exaltation and the rebuking of the Israelites, form one
of the most characteristic features of the Hebrew Bible.

This reminding by Muhammad of what the Bible says about the
Children of Israel is interspersed with Muhammad's own preaching,
pointing to them the deviations introduced which go against the
natural evolutionary course of religious concepts. They are told in
this unit not to be the first to deny the new message, which
confirms the revelations they have already about the worship of
God.

> O Children of Israel, remember the favour I have bestowed
> upon you. Keep your promise and I will be true to Mine;
> and of Me, of Me stand in awe. And believe in that I have
> sent down, confirming that which is with you, and be not
> the first to disbelieve in it. And do not barter away My
> messages for a trifling gain; and of Me, of Me be conscious.
> And do not overlay the truth with falsehood, and do not
> knowingly suppress the truth; and be constant in prayer,
> and spend in charity, and bow down in prayer with all who
> thus bow down.
>
> Would you enjoin righteousness on others and forget it
> yourselves, and yet you read the Book? Will you not, then,
> use your reason? And seek aid in steadfast patience and
> prayer: and this, indeed, is a hard thing for all but the
> humble in spirit who reckon that they shall meet their
> Lord and that unto Him they are returning.
>
> O Children of Israel, remember the favour I have be-
> stowed upon you, and how I favoured you above all other
> people; and beware of [the coming of] a Day, when no per-
> son shall in the least avail another, nor shall intercession be
> accepted from any of them, nor ransom taken from them,
> and none shall be helped.
>
> Remember how We delivered you from Pharaoh's peo-
> ple, who had oppressed you cruelly, slaying your sons and

sparing only your women, which was an awesome trial from Your Lord. And when We parted the sea for you and taking you to safety, drowned Pharaoh's men before your very eyes. And when We appointed for Moses forty nights [on Mount Sinai] and in his absence you took the worshipping of the [golden] calf, and thus became evildoers; yet even after that We pardoned you, so that you might have cause to be grateful.

And [remember] when We gave Moses the Book and [thus] the knowledge of right and wrong, so that you might be rightly guided; and when Moses said to his people: You have wronged yourselves my people in worshipping the calf; now turn to your Maker and slay one another. That will be better for you in your Maker's sight, and He will turn to you; truly He is the Forgiving One, the Merciful.

(Surah 2:40–54)

In the unit 3:187–188, they are told that by restricting the revelation to themselves (the exclusiveness of Judaism), they broke the pledge to make the revelation known to all mankind. This selfish behaviour in altering the direction of God's message is condemned.

And lo, God accepted a solemn pledge from those who were granted earlier revelation [when He bade them]: Make it known unto mankind, and do not conceal it. But they cast this [pledge] behind their backs, and bartered it away for a trifling gain: and how evil was their bargain. Think not that those who exalt in what they have thus contrived, and who love to be praised for what they have not done – think not they will escape suffering: for grievous suffering does await them [in the life to come].

(Surah 3:187–188)

In Surah 5:12–19, the Children of Israel are reminded of their breaking of the covenant, distortion of the meaning of the revealed words and removal from context, and abandonment of a good portion of the message they were supposed to convey to all mankind. Some of the followers of Jesus also forgot part of what they were supposed to transmit. The act of proclaiming that Jesus was the son of God is a denial of the truth.

77

Both Jews and Christians say that they are God's children and His beloved ones. They are told by Muhammad that they are human beings of God's creating, subject to God's forgiveness and to His punishment like everyone else. Both groups are invited to come to the new message.

God took compact with the Children of Israel; and we raised up from among them twelve chieftains. And God said: I am with you. Surely, if you perform the prayer, and pay the purification levy, and believe in my messengers and assist them, and lend God a good loan, I will acquit your evil deeds, and I will admit you to gardens watered by running streams. So whoever of you thereafter disbelieves, surely he has gone astray from the right way.

Then, for having broken their compact, We rejected them and caused their hearts to harden [so that now] they distort the meaning of the [revealed] words, taking them out of their context; and they have forgotten much of what they have been told to bear in mind; and from all but a few of them, you will never cease to light upon some act of treachery on their part. But pardon them, and forbear: verily, God loves the doers of good.

And [likewise] from those who say 'we are followers of Jesus', We took compact; and they have forgotten a portion of that they were reminded of. So We have stirred up among them enmity and hatred, till the Day of the Resurrection; and will assuredly tell them of the things they wrought. People of the Book now there has come to you Our Messenger, to make clear unto you much of what you have been concealing [from yourselves] of the Bible, and to pass over much.

O followers of the Book! Now there has come unto you from God, a light, and a clear Book, through which God shows unto all that seek His goodly acceptance the paths leading to salvation, and, by His leave, brings them out of darkness into the light and guides them onto a straight way.

Indeed, those who say: God is the Messiah, son of Mary, [they] deny the truth. Say: who then shall overrule God in any way if He desires to destroy the Messiah, Mary's son, and his mother, and all those who are on earth? For, God's is the dominion over the heaven and the earth and all that is between them; He creates what He wills: and God has the power to will anything.

And [both] the Jews and the Christians say: we are God's children, and His beloved ones. Say: why then does He chastise you for your sins? No, you are but human beings of His creating. He forgives whom He wills, and He chastises whom He wills. For God's is the dominion over the heavens and the earth and all that is between them, and to Him is the homecoming.

O people of the Book, now there has come to you Our Messenger, making things clear to you, upon an interval between the Messengers, lest you should say: there has not come to us any bearer of good tidings, neither any warner. Indeed there has come to you a bearer of good tidings and a warner; and God has the power to will anything.

(Surah 5:12–19)

In Surah 3:45–64, which will not be quoted here, the birth of Jesus is reported in such a manner as to suggest a supernatural occurrence. However, on closer analysis of the words it is clear that the birth is in fact natural. This is confirmed later in Surah 3:59, where it is asserted that the nature of Jesus is the same as that of Adam: he is a fully-fledged human being created from dust like every other human.

This sort of language is quite common in the Qur'an. In preaching the new message to the Christians and Jews, Muhammad tried his best to build upon what they already had but without being in conflict with the basis of the new message. It was not an easy task preaching to people of that age, still saturated with all sorts of beliefs which admitted of unnatural things happening in this life; hence the use of 'religious idiom' and veiled elliptical language.

The use of religious idiom gives the impression or appearance of still using the old religious language of supernatural happenings. However, on closer reading, one finds that this language in the Qur'an is linked simultaneously with the language of reason (see Chapter 5). The reason for this procedure is what I call the 'politics of preaching'. We shall encounter this discourse later when dealing with freedom of choice, where it is used for rhetorical and consolational reasons. Looking at the overall plan of the new message in the Qur'an and the uncovering of the politics of preaching, there is no escaping the conclusion that in this world, natural language prevails over 'religious idiom' language. The use of the device of linking religious idiomatic language and equating it with natural language usage serves as a key to unlock many apparent contradictions, as we will see in due course.

Similarly, elliptical language has been used in various situations in the Qur'an in addition to that reporting Jesus's birth and death. For example, it is used in the verses dealing with the election or choice to preach or indicate the way to God in Surah 3:33–34 and in Surah 2:130 and 2:124, alluded to earlier. Elliptical and veiled language is found also in other situations, for example concerning Solomon in Surah 27 or concerning Abraham in Surah 2:260. Finally, after relating the story of Jesus's mission and his rejection by the Jewish establishment, the people of the Book are told that a long period passed in which they did not have any messenger or warner; now, they have a bringer of a good tidings and a warner.

In the preaching to the Jews, three historical categories appear to be differentiated, which correspond to their occurrence in the Hebrew Bible. The first category concerns Abraham, his children and grandchildren. They are not regarded by the Qur'an as Israelites or Jews. They are what I call 'Arabaic', that is, Semitic tribes roaming their habitat. They are regarded by the Qur'an as natural worshippers of God at their time, using their natural disposition of pursuing the way of God in accordance with their empirical experience.

The second category concerns Moses and Aaron and the Children of Israel (the Israelites), who were rescued from the oppression of the Pharaoh of Egypt, according to the Hebrew Bible, and which the Qur'an describes for purposes of reminding. These Israelites are characterised by renegade behaviour and almost continual rebellion against Yhwh, as described in the Torah and other books of the Hebrew Bible such as Nehemiah 9. The Qur'an regards them as described in the Hebrew Bible, but they are the product of the third category.

The third category concerns the 'Jews' and corresponds to the time of Ezra (and Nehemiah) and afterwards, to which the Jewish audience of Muhammad belonged. According to the Hebrew Bible, Ezra is associated with bringing the Torah to Jerusalem in the Persian period. Only after that time did the term 'Jew' start to be used. 'Jew' is a corrupted form of Yehudi, signifying originally a resident of the district of Yehud; however, later it came to signify a follower of the religion of Judaism.

The Qur'an associates Ezra with 'Jews' in the verse (9:30) which says: 'The Jews say Uzair (diminutive of Ezra) is the son of God.'

This is symbolic, because Ezra is credited with bringing the Torah to Jerusalem and was put almost on a par with Moses. As the Hebrew Bible takes the collective 'Israel' as the son of God,[5] the Qur'an reports that the Jews of Muhammad's time regarded Ezra as the symbol of 'Israel'. This is not far-fetched in view of the position Ezra holds in the development of Judaism. This category is characterised by the Qur'an as altering the contents and changing the direction of the natural course of religious concepts by restricting the religious message to a single group of people. They claim their God exclusively for themselves. For more on this claim, it is best to go to the Hebrew Bible itself to see the position of 'Israel' in relation to Yhwh, the God of Israel.

5

THE OVERALL PLAN OF
THE QUR'AN FOR
MANKIND

We look next at the statements enunciated in the Qur'an which form the overall plan of the new message. These pertain to mankind's position on earth in this life, the purpose of this life, preparation for the task entrusted to mankind, the guidance provided, the granting of freedom of choice generally and of religion in particular, and the raising of the dead and the Day of Judgement.

Devolution of authority to mankind on earth

What does the Qur'an say about the position of man on earth? The answer is given in the following statements.

> And when your Lord said to the angels: *I am establishing upon the earth a successor (khaleefah)*. They replied: will You put there one who will do corruption and shed blood, while we are going swimmingly and gratefully to Your desire and are in dedication to You. He said: assuredly I know what you do not know. And He taught Adam the names, all of them; then He presented them unto the angels and said: now tell me the names of these, if you speak truly. They replied: continuous obedience to You (literally swimmingly performing your order) we have no knowledge except that You have taught us. You are the All-knowing and All-wise. Then He said: O Adam, inform them of the names of these [things]. And when Adam had named them, He (God) said: did I not tell you that I alone know the hidden reality of the heavens and the earth and all that you bring in the open and all that you would conceal.
>
> (Surah 2:30–37)

It is He who appointed you successors in the earth. Hence, he who is bent on denying the truth [ought to know that] his denial of his will fall back upon him ...

(Surah 35:39)

It is He who has appointed you successors in the earth and has raised some of you in rank above others, that He may try you in what He has given you; verily your Lord is swift in punishment, but He is also forgiving and merciful.

(Surah 6:165)

Surely worthier is He who answers the constrained when he calls unto Him and relieves the affliction [that caused the constraint] *and appointed you to be successors in the earth*; what! a god with God? How little indeed you reflect.

(Surah 27:62)

What does 'successor' mean in these verses? The verb *khalafa*, from which the noun *khaleefah* in the first quoted passage is derived, means 'to come after', 'to succeed', 'to take the place of'. In the next three quoted passages, the plural of *khaleefah* is used in each. In the first passage, Adam, which stands for mankind, is appointed by God as [His] successor on earth.

In passages 2–4, the addressees are human beings in general, as the plural and the general context indicate. In these units, mankind is being reminded of its special position in which it has been placed, by God. The verb *khalafa* is a common one, which is used in the Qur'an many times in various forms; it is used in the same sense in everyday speech. A few examples will suffice to illustrate this.

And We appointed a meeting with Moses for thirty nights which We completed with ten other nights, so that his whole time with His Lord amounted to forty nights. And Moses said to his brother Aaron: *Be my successor (take my place) among my people* and act rightly and do not follow the way of the corrupters.

(Surah 7:142)

The imperative verb is being used here. Moses is essentially telling his brother: be in charge, while I am away.

The verb 'to succeed' or 'to replace' is applied to money in the following verse:

Say: my Lord indeed outspreads and straitens His provisions to whomsoever He wills of His servants; and whatever it be you shall spend [on charity], *He will replace it*; He is the best of providers.

(Surah 34:39)

In Surah 38:26, the word 'successor' is applied to a specific person, with the meaning of 'being in charge'. It says:

O David, *We have made you a successor in the land* (i.e. a ruler or master) so judge between (rule) people with justice and do not follow the desires (lust), lest it lead you astray from the path of God. Surely those who go astray from the way of God, there awaits them a terrible chastisement, for that they have forgotten the Day of Reckoning.

In an argument with Muhammad, the Meccans pointed out that worshipping their gods to bring them nearer to Allah is no different from the worship of Jesus by the Christians. The reply in the Qur'an said that Jesus was no more than a blessed servant made to be an example for the Children of Israel. Then the verse 43:60 follows:

Had We so willed, We would have appointed angels among you *to be successors in the earth.*

Here the imperfect verb is used. The context of angels here refers to the belief that the goddesses the Meccans worshipped were female angels called the daughters of Allah. There are more examples in the Qur'an using *khalafa* and its derivatives.

It is worth noting that when Muhammad died, a new leader of the Muslim community was appointed who was called the successor (*khaleefah*) of the Messenger of God. Finally, the verb *khalafa* and its derivatives are used today in everyday speech in the same sense. For example, one's progeny are called *khilfah*, that is, what one leaves behind (the children, the heirs). The usage of this verb (to succeed or to replace) is very old, and it can be seen in the Hebrew Bible (for example, Genesis 41:14; Psalm 102:27; Job 14:14), in the Dead Sea Scrolls[1] and the Mesha Inscription (*wa-yakhlifoh*, i.e. and [his son] succeeded him).[2]

We may conclude that the statement in Surah 2:30 means what it says; that God put mankind in full charge on earth. This empowerment or mandate with full responsibility runs during the sojourn of man on earth (in this witnessable world) and ends upon his death. This is stressed throughout the Qur'an, as illustrated by Surah 7:24–25, which says: 'You have the earth for an abode for a while, wherein you live and die; and from it you will be taken out.'

The Qur'an announces in many places the eventual end of this devolution of power to mankind and their return to God to give account of their mandate on earth. Examples are:

> And let not those who are niggardly with the bounty God has given them, let them not suppose it is better for them. No, it is worse for them; that they were niggardly with, they shall have hung around their necks on the Resurrection Day. And to God belongs the inheritance of the heavens and the earth; and God is aware of the things you do.
>
> (Surah 3:180)

> Surely We shall inherit the earth and that upon it, and unto Us they shall be returned.
>
> (Surah 19:40)

> It is We who ordain life and death, and it is We who are the Heir of all things.
>
> (Surah 15:23)

> And We shall inherit from him what he is [now] saying, and he shall come before Us all alone.
>
> (Surah 19:80)

The addressee here is a single person. Not only the persons are returned to God but also all what they have said (and done).

It is of interest to note the words used for the termination of devolution of power to mankind. It is not God who is returning to collect His inheritance, but it is man who is returned to God.

God's creation at the disposal of mankind to utilise

Not only did God put mankind to be in charge on earth in this life, He also put at their disposal for their utilisation all that is in the heavens and that is in the earth; in other words, all natural phenomena. There are many verses in the Qur'an which point to this. A few examples follow.

> It is God who has made the sea subservient to you, so that ships might sail through it at His behest, and that you may seek to obtain [what you need] of His bounty and that you might have cause to be grateful. And He has made subservient to you, all that is in the heavens and on earth. Surely in that, there are signs for a people who think.
>
> (Surah 45:12–13)

> Are you not aware that God has subjected to you all that is in the heavens and all that is on earth, and He lavished on you His blessings, both outward and inward.
>
> (Surah 31:20)

> He has forced the night and the day, and the sun and the moon, into your service; the stars also are subjected [to you] by His command. Surely in this there are signs for people who use their reason. And it is He who made the sea subservient, so that you might eat fresh flesh from it, and bring forth out of it ornaments for you to wear; and you may see the ships ploughing their course through its waters. All this He has created, that you may seek His bounty and thus have cause to be grateful.
>
> (Surah 16:12, 14)

Thus we are reminded that all our existence is dependent on the utilisation of the natural phenomena, God's creation. We only utilise and transform; we do not create.

The aim of mankind's empowerment and mandate

What is the aim of the devolution of authority to man during this life on earth? The answer is given in several places in the Qur'an. For example:

1   In Surah 6:165 above, we are told that God devolved power to man so that He might try him by means of what He bestowed upon him.

2   In Surah 76:2, it is declared that the human being was created and endowed with discerning faculties so that he might be put to the proof.

3   Another verse, Surah 21:35, says: 'Every person is bound to taste death, and We try you with evil and good for a testing, and to Us you shall be returned.'

4   Surah 18:7 says: 'Verily, We have made all that is on earth as its adornment be a means by which We put men to a test, [showing] which of them are best in conduct.'

5   It is declared in Surah 67:1–2: 'Hallowed be He in Whose hands all dominion rests, Who has the power over all things. He Who created death as well as life, so that He may put you to a test [and thus show] which of you is best in conduct; He is the All-mighty, the All-forgiving.'

6   It is stated in Surah 2:148: 'Each one has a goal towards which he turns. Therefore vie with one another in doing good works. Wherever you may be, God will bring you all together, surely God has power over all things.'

Here we are told life is like a competition, and we are urged to compete with one another in doing good works on an individual and national level. The good works prescribed by the Qur'an are all related to expending some of what one cherishes for the benefit of mankind (society). In Surah 51:56–58 we are told that God created all (*jinn* and humans, that is, the unfamiliar and the familiar beings respectively) just to serve Him and that He desires of them no provisions or food. Thus the essence of service or worship of God involves being conscious of Him to avoid the following of excessive selfish tendencies and doing good works in society.

The aim of this mandate is quite clear. It is a trial. During this period of trial, mankind are wholly responsible for running the show in this life. They have been given full authority. This, of course, is in line with the empirical fact that man is the actor on earth and everything in human affairs, good or evil, has been done directly by humans, keeping in mind the basis of inspiration and learning (see below).

The learning process (inspiration or revelation): the basis of knowledge

Has the human being been prepared for this task with which he is entrusted? Man has been equipped for this mandate with the basic tools necessary on two levels: the material level used for observation and the non-material one used for understanding and conceptualisation. This preparation or initiation which we met in Surah 30:30 is detailed here. The material tools to be used have been mentioned in several places in the Qur'an, often along with the non-material. Examples are:

1   'We created the human being from a drop of mingled sperm in order to try him, thus We made him a being endowed with hearing and seeing' (Surah 76:2).
2   'It is He who endowed you with hearing, sight and hearts (minds), yet how little gratitude you show' (Surah 23:78).
3   'Say: [God is] He who has brought you [all] into being and has endowed you with hearing and sight and hearts, [yet] you are seldom grateful' (Surah 67:23).
4   'And God has brought you forth from your mother's womb knowing nothing and He endowed you with hearing and sight and minds so that you might have cause to be grateful' (Surah 16:78).

The material (i.e. visible) tools are the instruments of hearing and seeing, while the figurative tool used for understanding is the heart (mind or intellect). The first two are easily discernible. However, the third faculty, the 'heart', is more general and figurative. Literally, 'heart' means what is inside the body and is involved in the process of understanding or perception. Another word used in the Qur'an which carries this general meaning and used in the same context is *albaab*, the plural of *lubb* or *labab*, which means heart, the 'inside' or essence. It is involved in abstract discernment and understanding. Examples of the use of *albaab* are found in Surahs 3:7, 3:190, 14:52, 38:29 and elsewhere.

The Qur'an uses 'heart' also in the sense of a 'container of thoughts', as for example in Surah 2:204. It is also used as the receptor or the seat of inspiration, as in Surah 26:192–195. When the heart is blocked, no understanding (for example, 9:87, 17:46) or inspiration (for example, 42:24) is possible. In Surah 2:225, the hearts are endowed with the activities of thinking which might lead to righteous or evil deeds.

This figurative seat of understanding and perception is related in this study to the presence in the human being of the Spirit of God. It is the element responsible for the susceptibility of any human to become inspired under the right conditions. That is the ability to go beyond the mere observation of happenings, or the listings and cataloguing of information or data. It is the ability to pursue an invisible thread connecting the observed events or data together and form a mental picture of the interconnectedness of what has been observed, that is, the ability to conceptualise. The totality of using this process (observation and conceptualisation) is called the following of the 'upright religion or way', the use of the right frame of mind or of the natural disposition God initiated or originated humans with in the first instance (see 6:79 and 30:30). It is clear that the 'upright religion' in Surah 30:30 and implied in Surah 6:79 and other verses stressing the following of the right direction in life (such as 2:112, 3:83 and 4:125) indicates here a mental orientation or attitude to which humans have been disposed or initiated with in the process of creation.

A permanent element has been installed in the human being by God, according to the Qur'anic creation units, when humanity appeared on earth. Clearly this reflects the development of the conscious mind in humans. God addresses the angels in Surahs 15:29 and 38:72: 'And when I have formed him fully and breathed into him of My spirit, fall you down before him in prostration.' In Surah 32:9, both the material and figurative tools as well as the basic or spiritual element are combined together: 'and then He shaped him and breathed into him of His spirit, and He endowed you with hearing, sight, and hearts: What little thanks do you return?'

The non-material (invisible) element (rooh, translated above as 'spirit') which was breathed into the human being by God is recognised here as the invisible thread, link or element which is involved in consciousness and the inspiration process when the right conditions are obtained. Several instances in the Qur'an point to this use of spirit (rooh) as inspiration. Examples of this follow.

> He sends down the angels with the *inspiration* of His Command upon whomsoever He wills among His servants (creatures) bidding them to proclaim: there is no God but I (i.e. One Ultimate Reality); so be conscious of Me.
>
> (Surah 16:2)

> High above all orders of [being] is He, in almightiness en-throned. By His own will, does He bestow *inspiration* upon whomever He wills of His servants, so as to warn [all hu-

man beings of the coming] of the Day when they shall
meet Him.

(Surah 40:15)

And thus We have at Our behest sent *inspiration* to you
[Muhammad], when you knew nothing of the Book, or
faith, but [now] We have caused this [message] to be a
light, whereby We guide whom We will of Our servants;
and verily you too shall guide [people] onto the straight
path.

(Surah 42:52)

It is they in whose hearts He has inscribed faith, and whom
He has strengthened with *inspiration* from Himself.

(Surah 58:22)

This non-material (invisible) element God installed in the
human being is part and parcel of our make-up. It is the basis of our
ability to agree on (the unprovable) ground rules or axioms which
are preliminarily assumed as our starting points in any given field
of knowledge, where we accept them eventually as *reasonable*. It is
also considered as the driving force for going beyond the mere
observations of phenomena, and is involved in the unannounced
initial step in scientific research, the seeking to understand or look
for an order in a seemingly chaotic information or data. It is like an
'automatic pilot' installed in human beings to help them seek the
invisible threads interconnecting the observed events (data). Thus
the material tools used for the observations, together with the
ability to become inspired and go beyond the observed data, form
the basis of the learning process. This is mankind's only tool for the
mandate in this life on earth. Our knowledge, gained through this
learning process, is continuously expanding. It expands by utilising
the empirical observations and trying to go beyond the observations
using our imagination. Any picture generated from the
'imaginative' process which does not go along or fit the empirical
observation (experience) is usually discarded once that is shown to
be so beyond any reasonable doubt. This is usually accompanied by
the eventual emergence of a new mental picture which goes along
with experience better than the old picture. In the Qur'anic
terminology or religious idiom, the term used for discarding an old
mental picture or an old conceptual model is 'abrogating' or
'erasing'. This process of discarding (erasing) and confirming

(establishing) mental pictures (concepts) or 'books' goes on *ad infinitum* until the end of the mandate.

It must be pointed out here that Surah 2:31 does not indicate that Adam was taught the true nature of things, but rather the names of things, as the surah specifies. This means that the knowledge gained empirically is relative and not absolute, as is obvious from our initial axiomatic step upon which we build our analysis of our observations in any field of knowledge. The Qur'an stresses that seeking God or God's way in this life is through observing, examining and reflecting upon the creation, the natural phenomena (the signs of God), as has already been emphasised. This is clearly stated in Surah 31:29–30:

> Are you not aware that it is God who causes the night to enter into the day and makes the day enter into the night and He has subjected the sun and the moon [to laws by which] each speeds to a stated term and that God is fully aware of all what you do? *That is because God is the Truth* and that what they call besides Him is the falsehood.

(The phenomenon of the day entering into the night and vice versa refers to the variations of the lengths of the days and of the nights during the year.) The truth which is being sought continuously by humans in this life will become fully manifest at the Day of Reckoning as declared in Surah 24:25: 'Upon that day, God will pay them in full their just due, and they shall know that God is the manifest truth.'

All our knowledge is based on empirical observations of our surroundings, the natural phenomena, physical or otherwise. We learn to utilise these phenomena for good or evil, but never learn the true nature of things, although we continually try to form and reform a mental picture in the attempt to arrive at the truth.

The expansion of our knowledge and experience may be pictured as follows: if we imagine the expansion of our knowledge as an expanding bubble wherein we reside, then as a result of our increasing knowledge the inner surface is pushed outwards from the inside. This expansion will continue as long as we are gaining knowledge, until the end of the mandate of mankind in this world when the bubble will eventually burst and we are released and reality appears. It is to be noted that the Qur'an uses the ubiquitous (mentioned more than two hundred times) religious idiom 'God sending down' to refer to the Book, the Qur'an, the remembrance, the angels, the Torah, the Evangel, wisdom, and so on, to His servants (creatures). An example is the second verse in Surah 32 quoted below. This 'sending down' refers to the process of inspiration (revelation) just described as a result of the activation of that 'non-material' bond or element God installed in the human being. It is not that God is 'sending down' a physical book, a lump of matter already inscribed, but it is the human being activating the link with God (that is, applying reason and imagination on the observations or experiences in question) to achieve the inspiration which produces the contents of the Book (Surah 13:38).

Thus in reality, inspiration or revelation is a human activity connected with the learning process and the seeking of the truth. There is an invisible thread connecting things together (the Order) and humans struggle to delineate this invisible interconnectedness. The effort lies with the human being. This invisible interconnectedness points the way to God, the ultimate reality. The process of inspiration or revelation need not only deal with large issues such as man's destiny, but may deal with something mundane such as inventing a new tool, discovering a new product or solving any simple problem, regardless of how trivial it may appear. This can be clearly seen in Surah 57:25:

> We have sent Our messengers with clear signs (messages) and We sent down with them the Book and the scales of justice so that men may conduct themselves with fairness. And We sent down iron, wherein is great might, and many uses for people.

In the first part of the verse, the 'sending down', or the inspiration (revelation), refers to matters which come generally under the term religion dealing with the aim and meaning of life and the preaching of social justice. In the second part of the verse, the 'sending down' refers to the discovery of iron and its technological utilisation in times of war and peace.

Thus we find here another important linkage between the 'religious idiom', which gives the impression that everything appears to be directly done by God, and the naturalistic language which mirrors empirical experience and knowledge and reflects human activity. The linkage here is through the use of the same 'sending down' process, for two entirely different situations or products. In the first situation, the sending down of a Book, one automatically thinks of the religious idiom; in the second, the sending down of iron, one automatically thinks of human empirical experience. Both of these situations are equated. This linking smooths the transition from the use of the old 'religious idiom', which was practically the 'official' language of religious discourse and which is still entrenched in everyday speech even in modern times, to the use of the rational natural language based on human empirical observations (experience). Another example of using the religious idiom of 'God sending down' something that humans eventually discovered is illustrated in Surah 7:26:

> O children of Adam, We have 'sent down' on you a garment to cover your nakedness as well as a thing of beauty (literally plummage), but the garment of God-consciousness (piety) – this is best; that is one of God signs, perhaps they will reflect.

The revelation here is the discovery of clothing. The evolutionary development of clothing is linked or balanced with an abstract sort of clothing which envelops human beings, namely God-consciousness. Again, this emphasises the unity of material and abstract revelations.

The religious idiom, the 'sending down' process or 'inspiration or revelation', is generalised in Surah 15:21: 'Naught is there, that does not have its source with Us, and We *send it not down* but in a known measure (or a quantified amount).' This indicates that the invisible thread going through all things in the creation ends with God. Thus gaining knowledge and learning is like getting hold of one end of the invisible thread at the lowest level and proceeding to higher levels. Eventually, according to this, the end of the road would be reached leading us to God. Reaching the end of the thread would correspond to the bursting of the bubble in the analogue mentioned earlier. The Qur'an tells us that at the end of the road, a veil or a cover will be removed from our eyes (Surah 50:22) so that we 'shall know that God is the manifest Truth' (Surah 24:25).

The second part of the above statement from Surah 15:21 tells us that inspiration, the religious idiom of sending down, is quantified. That is, our effort to advance our knowledge occurs in steps of definite amounts. This aspect of quantification has been emphasised to be applicable to everything in the creation, as for example in Surahs 13:8, 25:2, 54:49 and 65:3. This common ground between the general creation and human deliberations has also been emphasised through the use of the verb *fatara*. For example, God is described as the Originator (the Creator) of the heavens and the earth in Surahs 6:14, 12:101, 14:10, 35:1, 39:46 and 42:11. In these verses the active participle of *fatara*, *faater(u)*, is used for the creation of the heavens and the earth, which is similar to the use of the verbal noun *fitrah* in Surah 30:30, where it is applied to 'religion', the natural disposition to seek the truth.

The meaning indicated in Surah 30:30 gives the impression that 'religion', the natural tendency to seek the way of God (the truth), is seeded in the creation and would spring out in humanity like a new growth from a germinating seed breaking (or cleaving) the surface of the soil (or like a chick breaking out from the shell of the egg). It is of interest to note here that the same word, *fitrah*, is used in the Hebrew Bible for a newborn 'breaking out' from the womb, for humans and animals alike.[3]

The meaning alluded to above for *fatara* and its verbal noun *fitrah* in Surah 30:30, as well as that in the Hebrew Bible, must also apply generally to the use of the active participle *faater* in the creation of the system of the universe, heavens and earth. This means that the system is also initiated or born with an inbuilt tendency or information, like any newborn 'breaking out' from the package of its inception. This general initiation with the information package, which acts as the driving force in the course of life, is related to what we have called earlier the *tasbeeh*, or the intensive flow or swimming of everything in the universe towards God. This 'flow towards God' is voluntary for human deliberations, which is related to human consciousness centred around freedom of choice, and involuntary for purely material systems. There is an intermediate consciousness in animals. The Qur'an also uses the derivative of *fatara* in its literal sense, as in *futoor* in Surah 67:3 to mean cracks,[4] breaks or flaws in the heavens, and also as in Surah 82:1 – 'when the heavens are rent asunder' (*infatarat*) – in describing the coming of the Day of Judgement.

Finally, it is worth mentioning a statement in Surah 33:40, which has a bearing on revelation and prophethood. This declares that 'Muhammad ... is the seal (the last) of the prophets'. This must not be viewed as if 'The Holy Spirit' would be departing from mankind and inspiration ceasing at Muhammad's death, or as God severing or blocking the bond between Him and humanity. But, in view of what has already been discussed, it must be regarded as a declaration of the ending of the classical era of 'prophecy'. This is because Muhammad removed the element of secrecy or magic from the process of the so-called 'prophecy', by pointing out the general methodology which can be used to receive inspiration. In essence, this methodology 'secularised' inspiration or revelation. Inversely, the methodology of the Qur'anic discourse consecrated and spiritualised the rational or 'scientific' method, to put it into modern terminology. Thus, concluding this section, inspiration (revelation) will continue in all matters large or small but without being couched in the usual 'religious idiom', and the person being inspired is no longer called a 'prophet' of God.

Guidance: the showing of the two ways

Is there anything else needed for the journey? Is not the 'automatic pilot' sufficient for guiding a human being during his lifetime? The answer is given in the creation units in the Qur'an. When Adam was appointed by God to be 'successor' on earth, the angels objected to this appointment, protesting that Adam would be spreading corruption and shedding blood on earth. However, their objection was overcome after they realised that, unlike them, Adam had something they lacked, namely the ability to learn, which goes beyond what they were taught (or instructed) by God. This was explained in the previous section as due to the presence of the Spirit of God in Adam.

So the angels obeyed God and fell down in prostration to Adam, except for one of them, Iblees, who refused and swelled in pride, saying: 'I am nobler than he (Adam). You created me from fire, but him from clay' (Surah 38:76). This marks the birth of selfish behaviour and the appearance of the 'I am better than' attitude. This angel was then demoted from the angelic state, which the Qur'an characterises by a state where angels move swimmingly to God's command (desire) by performing their routine or assigned courses (for example, Surah 2:30). After pleading with God to defer his judgement and allow him to stay free within humanity, he was given his choice and Iblees's fate became linked with that of Adam to be decided at the Day of Judgement.

It is to be noted here that 'Iblees' will be called from now on in the Qur'an by the name Satan, a descriptive epithet arising from his activity: enticing, seducing, whispering in people's ears and hearts, and so on. Satan swore that he would try to seduce human beings and make them deviate from the way of God. He swore to embellish the things which the humans have been recommended to avoid and make such things look good and so deceive them. The exceptions will be God's sincere servants, who are able to withstand

Satan's pressure. There are many verses in the Qur'an dealing with Satan's activities. The following unit covers most of the items mentioned above (Surah 38:71–85):

> [For,] lo, your Lord said unto the angels: Behold, I am about to create a human being out of clay; and when I have formed him fully and breathed into him of My spirit, fall you down before him in prostration. Thereupon the angels prostrated themselves, all of them together, save Iblees who gloried in his arrogance, and [thus] became one of those who deny the truth. [God] said: O Iblees, what has kept you from prostrating yourself before that [being] which I have created with My hands? Are you too proud [to bow], or are you of those who think [only] of themselves as high? Answered [Iblees]: I am better than he: You have created me out of fire, whereas You created him out of clay. [God] said: Go forth, then, from this [angelic state] – for, behold, you are henceforth accursed, and My rejection shall be your due, until the Day of Judgement. Said [Iblees]: Then, O My Lord, grant me a respite till the Day when they shall be raised from the dead. [God] said: Verily, so [be it:] you shall be among those who are granted respite till the Appointed Day.
>
> Whereupon [Iblees] said: then [I swear] by Your very Might: I shall most certainly beguile them all into grievous error, [all] save such of them as are truly Your servants. And [God] said: This then is the truth, and this truth do I state: Most certainly will I fill hell with you and such of them as shall follow you, all together.

Thus we see another factor emerging. The road towards God comes under the influence of an invisible force (the satanic force) within humans themselves, which tends to deflect them from that path. (See Surah 114, where Satan is described as the whisperer in the hearts of all humans.) It appears from the contexts of the Qur'anic statements that the satanic influence represents the evil tendencies in the human thoughts and the excessive following of the desires (lust), all originating from selfishness. What then is the right way?

The right way is that which leads towards God. It is a direction or a frame of mind which leads a person to carry out such actions as described below. The Qur'an uses the term 'seeking the face (direction) of God'.

In Surah 90, God says:

> Have We not given him (the human being) two eyes and a tongue and two lips, and shown him the two high-ways [of good and evil]? Yet he did not attempt to ascend (assault) the steep uphill path (a barrier to be surmounted).
> And do you know what the steep uphill path is? [It is] the freeing of a human being from bondage or the feeding upon a day of hunger: of an orphaned relation, or of a needy person in misery; then, that he become of those who believe and counsel each other to be steadfast and counsel each other with compassion. Those are the people of the right [way].

(Surah 90:8–18)

What is important here in this description is that the 'right way' is an uphill way, not an easy way. The specific actions quoted above (see also Surah 2:177) are related to the welfare of human beings in society, a condition relevant at all times although the mechanism of rectifying the ills of society will vary with the times. All the specific deeds mentioned above are carried out by people who cannot be described, relative to other human beings, as self-centred. The implication is that the opposite way is a downhill way, an easy way, trodden by self-centred people with no concern for others. To follow the right way needs the expenditure of some effort. A barrier has to be surmounted. This effort is the moral or psychological work expended in countering and moderating the excesses of the selfish tendencies (lust) in human beings such as the lust for power, wealth, sex, and so on. We have already seen indications to actions which are righteous in the statement of Surahs 2:177 and 89 and in Surah 30 above (quoted in full in the appendix).

There are many similar urgings and indications to righteous deeds dispersed in the various surahs of the Qur'an, all involving moral effort to carry out. Carrying out such actions provides a moral elevation to the person performing them. What about those who do not attempt to assault or climb the uphill highway? These are described in the verses that follow.

Whereas those who are bent on denying the truth of Our messages (signs), they are such as have lost themselves in evil (the opposite of the right way), [with] fire closing in upon them.

(Surah 90:19–20)

Denying the truth of the message of God, that is, abandoning the right way or going astray, is associated in the Qur'an with following one's lust, the pursuance of excessive selfish desires. There are many such statements in the Qur'an, for example in Surahs 6:56, 6:150, 18:28, 20:16, 28:50, 38:26, 42:15, 45:23 and elsewhere, connecting the following of lust with deviation from the right path. One example follows:

> Tell them of the man to whom We gave Our messages, but he passed them by (departed from them), so Satan followed after him, and he became one of those who went astray (i.e., seduced from the right path). And had We willed [by not granting him the freedom of choice] We would have elevated him; but he inclined towards the earth and succumbed to his own excessive selfish desires (lust)....
> (Surah 7:175–176)

The above quote tells us that those who succumb to their lust are not elevated morally. This is because no moral work is expended to moderate and check their pursuit of their selfish desires. The pulling down towards the ground is accelerated and a moral fall results. Again we note the linkage between the 'religious idiom' and the natural language of human experience. In the first part of the statement, it appears that God willed the man to go astray; in the latter part we find it is the man's choice of action which led him astray. This is a generalisation which will be stressed later in this chapter in the discussion on freedom of choice: God's will concerning human actions reflects what humans choose to do.

Now the two highways have been indicated. Taking the right path involves controlling and moderating the desires, and leads to order and peace in society. This may be looked upon as using the full spectrum of the forces in the human psyche, giving a balanced behaviour and not allowing the forces governing selfish tendencies to predominate. Taking the way of desires, one lets the unchecked selfish desires take over, which leads to disorder and eventual fall of society.

What else is needed to make the Judgement of human beings at the end of the mandate fair? But before that a few words about the possible meaning of *jinn* as understood by this author from its context in the Qur'an and the literal meaning of the probable Semitic root.

Jinn *in the Qur'an*

The subject of *jinn* is usually treated in a unitary fashion, taking *jinn* as spiritual beings capable of doing all sorts of supernatural things, with a lot of extraneous conceptions included; these were developed by later generations. However, there is one treatment by Sayyed Ahmad Khan in the latter part of the nineteenth century in which he divested the concept of *jinn* of all supernatural and superstitious elements.[5] He held that the word *jinn* in the Qur'an referred to Bedouins and to other uncivilised and uncultured people.

In this study we note two contexts for the term *jinn*. One relates to local deities of persons, places and things which were prevalent in the Eastern Mediterranean region (the *genii* of the Romans, the *daemones* of the Greeks and their Semitic equivalents). The other context seems better related to human beings associated with some unfamiliarity as explained below.

We look first at the linguistic aspect of the term *jinn*. *Jinn* or *jinnah* is a collective noun which is derived from the verb *janna* = *janana*, which means to cover, conceal or hide, as vegetation or plants cover and shade the ground; hence the name *jannah* (for example, Surah 2:265–266) for a garden in Arabic. In the Hebrew Bible, *jan* or *jannah* are also used for a garden, for example in Genesis 2:15 and Isaiah 1:30, respectively. In Assyrian, *ginu* and also *gannatu* (both forms preserving the nominative ending) stand for garden. It is also found in Ugaritic as *gn* (unvocalised) to denote a garden.

In Isaiah 31:5, we see the use of the imperfect and the verbal noun in the same sentence, *yagin ... ganoon*, in which Yhwh, like flying birds, flies about invisibly covering or overshadowing Jerusalem and protecting her. In Arabic (and in Hebrew) *mijann* is a shield, an instrument which temporarily covers part of the body, making it invisible to the sword, spear or arrow of an enemy. *Junnah* means also a shelter or a screen. In all the above shades of meanings, the elements of covering and concealment are implied. It is in this sense that the verb *janna* is used in Surah 6:76 in the Qur'an: 'When the night covered him (i.e. it became dark because of the concealment of the sun) ... '

We propose to interpret the Qur'anic *jinn*, *jinnah* or *jaan*, basing our arguments on the meaning of the verb *janna* and on the Qur'anic context. Looking at the occurrences of the above terms, we find that they fall into two contexts. The first context implies non-material or spiritual beings (deities) which hence are intrinsically invisible. In this category we have the following occurrences:

Surah 55:15: 'And He created the *jaan* (*jinn*) from fire free of smoke.'

Surah 6:100: 'And they make the *jinn* partners with God ... '

Surah 18:50: 'And We told the Angels "prostrate yourselves before Adam". So they all prostrated themselves, except Iblees who was one of the *jinn*. But then he turned away from his Lord's command, will you then take him and his cohorts for [your] masters instead of me although they are enemies to you?'

Surah 34:40–41: 'One day He will gather them all together and will ask the angels, "was it you that these [men] used to worship?" They will answer: glory to You (literally vigorously and continuously we perform your command), You are our Master, apart from them; nay, but they were worshipping the *jinn*, most of them believed in them.'

What we gather from the above is that angels and *jinn* are non-material invisible spiritual beings, and that the *jinn* were worshipped by humans in association with God. There was a well-established pattern in the East Mediterranean region (and probably everywhere else as well) of worshipping local deities in addition to the higher Gods. These lower deities were the local gods of places (local sanctuaries), of persons (for example, as guardians) or of things (such as trees and springs). What is of interest to note at this point is that the Greeks called these lower deities *daemones* but the ancient Romans used the name *genii* (singular *genius*) for these natural gods of places, persons or things.[6] Thus we are forced to ask whether there is a relationship between the *jinn* of the Arabian Peninsula and the *genii* of the Romans. In view of the fact of the widespread influence of the Romans in the Near East, especially in the first few centuries of the common era when some Arabians at that time reached the highest position in the Roman hierarchy, we cannot rule out that possibility without further investigation. Regardless of the origin of the word *jinn* in this category and who influenced whom, the Romans or the Semites, the term refers to local deities.

The second context in which *jinn* occurs in the Qur'an is where we find both *ins* and *jinn* are mentioned together. *Ins* is a collective noun signifying humans, recognisable familiar human beings. It is derived from the verb *anisa* which means to be familiar with, to be in a state which is characterised by or affording occasion for agreeable conversation and friendliness and not instant hostility. The contexts in which both *ins* and *jinn* are mentioned together in the Qur'an indicate that *ins* and *jinn* are peoples subject to the same considerations such as temptations, belief and disbelief, forming nations, forming mixed alliances, having the same potential (Surah 55:33), having messengers of God sent to them, capable of being subjected to persecution and forced labour (Surah 34:14) and having all the usual desires such as male–female intercourse, and so on. The relevant verses are Surahs 6:112, 128, 130; 7:38, 179; 17:88; 27:17; 41:25, 29; 46:18, 29; 51:56; 55: 33, 39, 56, 74; and 72:1–6.

The difference between the *ins* and the *jinn* in this second context seems to reside only in the aspect of familiarity or lack of it, with *ins* being the familiar people, and *jinn* being the unfamiliar people. The people we are not familiar with, perhaps because they are living in far away places and are screened or shielded from our everyday vision, are *jinn*, which in modern terminology might be called foreign. However, unfamiliarity can even arise within the same country or land. The invisible covers or barriers responsible for unfamiliarity might be linguistic, a large difference in skill or in intellectual ability or even in class, which might produce a state of awe in the person lacking these qualities.

Jinnah is also used as a verbal noun signifying unfamiliarity or strangeness, as in Surahs 7:184, 23:25, 23:70, 34:8 and 34:46. *Jinnah* in the above verses is usually translated as madness due to being possessed by *jinn*. The Meccans accused Muhammad of having *jinnah* because he uttered things that were unfamiliar or strange to them (Surahs 7:184, 34:46 and elsewhere), and thus they called him *majnoon*, implying he was mad (for example in Surahs 15:6, 37:36 and 52:29).

The plural of *ins* is *unaas*, usually abbreviated for ease of pronunciation to *naas* (human beings), which is usually translated by Qur'anic translators as 'men'. This must be taken as figurative to signify familiar human beings, since there is an independent word for men as such (in contradistinction to women) which is also used in the Qur'an, for example in Surahs 2:282, 4:12, 4:34, 4:75, and so on. In fact, Surah 72:6 specifically mentions men of *jinn* and men of *ins*: 'But there were certain men of *ins* (familiar human beings) who would take refuge with certain men of the *jinn* (unfamiliar human beings), but these only made things worse (increased them in confusion) and they thought, even as you also thought, that God would never send forth anyone (i.e. as a messenger).'

In Surah 114, the word *al-naas* in verses 1–3 and verse 5 seems to indicate a generalisation of all humans, familiar and unfamiliar. In Surah 114:6 this generalised term is split into its two components: the unfamiliar human beings (the *jinnah* or *jinn*), and the familiar human beings (*al-naas*, the plural of *ins*). These two meanings for the same word used in this surah can only be deduced from the context.

We have seen above (in Surah 18:50) that Iblees, who is one of the *jinn*, was also one of the angels before his refusal to prostrate to Adam and his eventual demotion from the angelic state by being let loose (free) as a constant tempting force within the human being. So what is the angelic state? The concept of angels can only be glimpsed from the historical evolutionary development of the concept of God, as perceived by man, and the involvement in the control of nature, including living things. Humans first perceived different gods as controlling different aspects of nature. Then the idea of a chief god and lesser gods came into being, each performing certain functions. Eventually the lesser gods (and goddesses) became the sons (daughters) of the chief God until finally the sons (daughters) of God became angels of God, with the latter (angels) doing the jobs of the former (the sons of God).

Thus the concept of angels, which is a human conception, is connected with our perception of the creation and the control of natural phenomena, including man. This perception is a function of our experience. In the Qur'an, we are told about the angel of death, the angels assigned to individuals to keep records of what they say and do, and the mention of Mikael and Gabriel. The latter two clearly are related originally to El, the Chief Semitic deity. The Qur'an explicitly states that God made the angels to be messengers (Surah 35:1).

Perhaps one may conjecture that angels represent those forces that are involved in controlling and communicating with the creation. Iblees or Satan, then, based on this conjecture, represents that part of the spectrum of forces which are involved in the selfish tendencies in the human psyche. The full spectrum of forces in the human being contains other forces besides those responsible for the selfish tendencies, all of which are operative in the normal human.

No doubt we will be learning more and more about the forces controlling the various aspects of our behaviour in the future.

Freedom of choice and freedom of worship

The granting of freedom of choice to human beings is absolutely essential in order to fulfil the aim of the mandate on earth, namely: 'That He might put you to a test [and thus show] which of you is best in conduct.' The Qur'an (10:108) declares, addressing Muhammad:

> Say: O mankind, the truth has now come to you from your Lord. Whosoever chooses to follow the right path, follows it but for his own gain; and whosoever chooses to go astray, it is only to his own loss. I am not a guardian over you.

It is plainly stated in Surah 17:13–15:

> And every person's destiny We have tied to his neck (i.e., the person takes the direction or action he chooses) and on the Day of Resurrection We shall bring forth for him a record-book which he will find wide open; [and he will be told]: read your book, it suffices today that you yourself check your own account.
>
> Whoever chooses to follow the right path, follows it but for his own good; and whoever goes astray, it is only for his own loss; and no person shall bear another's burden ...

It is also clearly stated in Surah 6:104:

> Now clear insights have come to you from your Lord. Therefore whoso chooses to see, it is to his gain; and whoso chooses to remain blind, does so to his own hurt. And I [Muhammad] am not a keeper over you.

It is stated in Surah 27:89–93:

> Whoever shall come [before Him] with a good deed he shall have better than it; and they shall be secure from terror that day. And whoever comes with an evil deed, their faces shall be thrust in fire, [and they will be asked:] Is this not but a just reward for what you were doing [in life]?

[Say, O Muhammad:] I have only been commanded to serve the Lord of this city which He has made sacred; to Him belongs everything. And I have been commanded to be of those that submit [my face towards Him], and to proclaim the Qur'an. So whosoever chooses to follow the right path, follows it but for his own good; and if any wills to go astray, say [unto him]: I am only a warner.

Thus it is clear that the principle of 'freedom of choice' is paramount in the overall plan of the Qur'an. It is one of the cornerstones on which the Last Judgement is based. It is declared at several points in the Qur'an that God does not wrong human beings but humans wrong themselves by their actions. For example, Surah 10:44 says: 'Indeed, in no way does God wrong mankind, but humans wrong themselves.'

The Qur'an stresses that each person receives on the Day of Judgement what he or she earned with no injustice to any. In Surah 99:7–8, it says: 'Whoever does an atom's weight of good shall see it, and whoever does an atom's weight of evil shall see it.' There are many such statements in the Qur'an. In Surah 22:8–10, describing the punishment expected for a person who is bent on deflecting people from the path leading towards God, he is told to taste the chastisement for, 'what your own hands have brought forward; for never God is unjust to His creatures (servants).'

Finally, we quote a statement which proclaims the principle of freedom of choice in a manner which acts as a key to understanding many of the verses of the Qur'an which appear to contradict this principle and which give the impression that God forces humans to make their choices. This statement (in Surah 4:115) says: 'We shall turn him over [to the direction] he has already turned to.' That is to say, God will give a person what that person has already chosen. All statements which appear to be contradicting freedom of choice must be treated in the light of the above statement. We met this sort of Qur'anic discourse before when dealing with the politics of preaching and with learning and inspiration and guidance (Surah 7:175–176). Many of the apparently contradictory statements are rhetorical statements directed to Muhammad, mainly to console him.

Muhammad's overeagerness to bring his audience into the new faith and the resulting disappointments he suffered when rebuffed created many crises for him in the course of discharging his mission. This is discerned from the many relevant verses interspersed throughout the Qur'an, as already noted. In those situations Muhammad was told not to worry; it was not his fault and he could not make the blind see, or make the deaf hear. Therefore all the rebuffing he received is God's will; it is natural.

As God's will granted mankind the freedom of choice, those who rebuffed Muhammad exercised their option by denying Muhammad's message. Therefore everything is moving naturally. A few examples will illustrate this rhetoric directed to Muhammad.

First, in the course of arguing with Muhammad, his opponents accused him of inventing (forging) the Qur'an. Muhammad is told (Surah 10:38–44) to say that if he was able to invent the Qur'an, then why could not they devise just a single surah like it? Then the Qur'an continues:

> No, but they are bent on giving the lie to everything the wisdom thereof they do not comprehend, and before its inner meaning has become clear to them. Even so those that were before them cried lies; then behold how was the end of the evildoers. And some of them believe in it (the Qur'an), and some believe not in it; and your Lord knows best those who spread corruption. And [so] if they charge you with imposture, then say: My deeds are mine, and your deeds are yours. You are not accountable for my actions, nor am I accountable for what you do.
>
> Some of them [pretend to] listen to you, but can you cause the deaf to hear you, even though they will not use their reason? And there among them such as [pretend to] look towards you; but can you show the right way to the blind even though they cannot see? Indeed, in no way does God wrong mankind, but it is humans who wrong themselves.

Again in the following verses (6:33–35) the context is Muhammad's rebuff by his audience and also his impatience.

> We know too well that what they say grieves you. Yet it is not merely you whom they charge with falsehood, but the evildoers are denying God's messages. Other messengers have been denied before your time, yet they endured patiently with all those charges of falsehood, and all the hurt done to them, till Our help came unto them, for there is no power that could alter the decrees (words) of God.

And if it distresses you that those who deny the truth turn their backs on you, why, then, if you are able to go down deep in the earth or to ascend a ladder unto heaven in order to bring them a [yet more convincing] message, [do so;] but [remember that] had God so willed, He would indeed have gathered them all unto [His] guidance. Do not, therefore, be one of those who are ignorant [of God's way].

In the following verse (Surah 10:99) as in Surah 6:33–35 above, Muhammad is essentially being rebuked for his impatience and overeagerness in discharging his mission. It says:

And [thus it is] had your Lord so willed, all the peoples of the earth would have believed in Him, one and all (i.e., by not granting them freedom of choice). What! will you, then, compel people to become believers?

In the next passage (Surah 25:41–44), Muhammad is being told that it is useless and waste of time for him to persist preaching to some people who only mock him; they are like cattle, even worse.

Hence, whenever they see you, they but make you a target of mockery, saying: Is this the one whom God has sent as a Messenger? Indeed, he would well-nigh have led us astray from our gods, had we not been [so] steadfastly attached to them. But in time when they see the suffering [that awaits them], they will come to know who it was that went farther from the path [of truth].

Have you ever considered [O Muhammad, the kind of man] who makes his own desires (lust) his god? Could you, then, be held responsible for him? Or do you think that most of them listen [to your message] and use their reason? No, they are but like cattle; no, they are even less conscious of the right way.

This rhetoric is part of the Qur'anic discourse for the reasons mentioned above, and must be understood in the proper context. Those who deny the messages of God do so by choice and not forced into that position by God. This rhetoric became part of the psychological war of words between Muhammad and his opponents. Note the following discourse (Surah 2:8–18) which came at the height of Muhammad's difficulties with unbelievers and hypocrites:

There are some who declare: We believe in God and the Last Day, yet they are no true believers. They seek to deceive God and those who believe in Him: but they deceive none save themselves, though they may not perceive it. There is a sickness in their hearts which God has aggravated: they shall be sternly punished for the lies they tell. When they are told: Do not commit evil in the land, they reply: We do nothing but good. But it is they who are the evildoers, though they may not perceive it.

And when they are told: Believe as others believe, they reply: Are we to believe as fools believe? It is they who are the fools, if they but knew it. When they meet the faithful, they declare: We, too, are believers. But when alone with their satans (signifying human companions of similar evil impulses) they say to them: Verily, we are with you, we were only mocking. God will mock them, and shall lead them on blindly wandering in their insolence. [For] it is they who have purchased error in exchange of guidance; but their barter did not bring any gain, nor have they found guidance. The likeness of them is as the likeness of a man who kindled a fire, and when it lit all about him, God took away their light, and left them in utter darkness, wherein they cannot see: deaf, dumb, blind and they cannot return [to the right path].

Again this should not be confused with the clear statements of principle. In fact, this sort of discourse is now entrenched and has spread into everyday speech.

So far we have looked at the freedom of choice in the Qur'an in general. Of course this applies also to the freedom of worship, or choosing a religion as we already noted in Surah 109. A few more examples will be given to illustrate this point. For example, Muhammad is told in Surah 39:14–15 to declare: 'God alone do I worship, sincere in my faith in Him alone; and [it is up to you to] worship whatever you please instead of Him.'

In the course of his preaching to the Children of Israel, reminding them of Moses's mission and calling upon them to come to the new message, Muhammad is told in Surah 17:105–107:

In truth We sent it [the Qur'an] down, and with the truth it has come down. We have only sent you [Muhammad] to announce and to warn. We have parcelled out the Qur'an for you so that you might recite it to the people by stages (intervals), as We have sent it down piecemeal. Say: It is for you to believe in it or to deny it.

In Surah 23:117 it is declared:

Hence, he who invokes another god besides God, for whose existence he has no evidence, surely his reckoning shall be with his Lord; surely such deniers of the truth shall not achieve a happy state.

Another injunction addressed to Muhammad (Surah 18:29) says: 'And say: the truth [has now come] from your Lord. Let, then, him who will, believe in it; and let him who will, reject it ...' It says, whether you believe in the new message or you deny it, it is entirely up to you; but here are the consequences ...

Although the choice is that of the human being, nevertheless it must be emphasised that God is not indifferent to the choice taken, as can be seen from Surah 39:7 which declares:

If you are unthankful (by denying the truth), verily God has no need for you; none the less, He does not approve of ingratitude in His servants (creatures). But if you show gratitude, He will approve it in you ...

In the following, the freedom of religion is emphasised by a negative declaration (Surah 2:256). This says:

There shall be no coercion in matter of faith (religion). True guidance is now distinct from error. He that renounces the power of evil (error) and puts his faith in God, shall grasp a firm handle that is unbreakable. God hears all and knows all.

Again the consequences for the believers in, and the rejecters of, the truth are spelled out in the verses that follow the above quote.

We have already met situations quoted above where Muhammad was rebuked for being overzealous and told that he was only a warner, a messenger. It must be emphasised, however, that this Qur'anic protection of the freedom of choice and worship does not mean abandoning the freedom to preach to persons of different religions. Muhammad is told in Surah 16:125 to:

Invite to the way of your Lord with wisdom and with
kindly advice and dispute with them in the kindest manner. Verily your Lord knows best who stray from His way
and knows best who are rightly guided.

Diversity of beliefs recognised and regulated

This is stressed in many verses of the Qur'an. It comes in statements
saying that God will settle the disputes concerning different beliefs.
This is declared to forestall some humans from imposing beliefs on
others by using any means of force (physical, economical or
psychological). Muhammad is told to only warn, and that the
reckoning is left entirely to God at the Day of Judgement. More
examples follow. Muhammad is told in Surah 39:46 to say:

O God, Originator of the heavens and the earth, Knower of
all that is unwitnessable as well as of all that can be witnessed, it is You who will judge between your creatures
(people in general) in those matters about which they have
differed.

This has been also stressed in Surah 22:16–17, already quoted as
a unit, stating that God shall decide between the followers of
different religions at the Day of Judgement. This is proclaimed
again in slightly different manner in Surah 2:62, saying:

Verily they that believe and those of Jewry and the Christians and those Sabaeans, whoso believes in God and the
Last Day, and do what is right, their rewards await them
with their Lord, and fear shall not come upon them, neither shall they be grieved.

The above is repeated in Surah 5:69. Finally, I should point out
that in addition to the above, the Qur'an urges the various different
communities to: 'Vie with each other in good works, unto God you
shall all return, all together; and He will tell you of that whereon
you were at variance' (Surah 5:48).
This is the basis and the rule for coexistence between the various
communities and nations. It is stressed in the rest of the verse that
the above course is the right one, as different communities choose
different ways and cannot be forced into a single one because they

exercised their right to choose. It says: 'Had God willed [by not granting freedom of choice to mankind], He would have made you all one single community, but [He willed otherwise] in order to test you by means of what He has bestowed upon you. Therefore vie with each other in good works ... '

The return to God

This is one concept which permeates the whole Qur'anic discourse. It is a basic step in the plan propounded. We have already met it many times; a few more examples are given below.

Surah 28:88: 'Everything is bound to perish except His face, His is the judgement, and unto Him you shall be returned.'

Surah 23:115: 'What, did you think that We created you only for sport, and that you would not be returned to Us?'

Surah 29:57: 'Every human being is bound to taste death, then unto Us you shall be returned.'

Surah 3:83: 'What, do they seek another religion than God's, and to Him has surrendered whoso in the heavens and the earth, willingly and unwillingly, and to Him they shall be returned.'

Surah 11:123: 'To God belongs the unseen (the unwitnessable) in the heavens and the earth, and to Him the whole matter shall be returned.'

In the next unit everything is put in perspective: Muhammad's mission, the creation of the heavens and the earth and the celestial space between them, God's authority in governing the whole set-up of creation (what the Qur'an calls the Order, the Command), the creation of the human being from clay, making his reproduction in the manner known today, forming him, breathing into him of His spirit and endowing him with hearing, sight and heart (mind, perception, intellect). Yet humans tend to ignore their goal and their eventual encounter with their Lord. They are reminded that the angel of death will be visiting them and all shall be returned to God:

A. L. M. The sending down of the Book, issues, beyond any doubt, from the Lord of all the worlds. And yet, they [who are bent on denying the truth] assert that he [Muhammad] has invented it. No, but it is the truth from your Lord, enabling you [Muhammad] to warn [this] people to whom no warner has come before you, so that they might follow the right path.

It is God who has created the heavens and the earth and all that is between them in six days, and is established on the seat of power. You have none to protect you from God, and none to intercede for you [on Judgement Day], will you not reflect? He directs the Order (Command), from the celestial space (heaven) to the earth; and in the end all shall ascend unto Him on a Day the length thereof will be [like] a thousand years of your reckoning. Such is He, the knower of the unwitnessable and the witnessable, the Almighty, the Merciful, who makes most excellent every thing He creates. Thus, He originated the creation of the human being out of clay; then made his offspring from a drop of a humble fluid; and then He shaped him and breathed into him of His spirit, and He endowed you with hearing, sight, and hearts: what little thanks do you return?

For, [many are] they [who] say: What! after we have been [dead and] lost in the earth, shall we indeed be [restored to life] in a new act of creation? No, but [by saying this] they deny the truth that they are destined to meet their Lord. Say: [One day] the angel of death who has been given charge of you, will gather you, and then unto your Lord you will be brought back.

(Surah 32:1–11)

According to the Qur'an everything in the creation, and not only humans and their deliberations, moves smoothly and obediently (literally, swimming intensively) towards God (Surahs 57:1, 59:1, 61:1, 24:41 and elsewhere), but 'you [humans] do not understand their obedient motion (their intensive swimming) [to God]' (Surah 17:44). The verb used in the Qur'an for this motion towards God is the intensive form of 'to swim', reflecting an intensive action. It is applied in the usual form 'to swim' to the motion of the night and day and the moon and the sun in their orbits (Surahs 21:33 and 36:40). The intensive form of the verb 'to swim' is usually translated 'to glorify, to praise'; however, we must not forget its literal meaning which seems to give a more appropriate meaning to describe the motion towards God with gratitude.

The whole Order (Affair) in this universe ascends to God, taking a very long time. The time given in Surah 32:1–11 above, one thousand years, is only figurative. In Surah 70:3 the figure is even greater, fifty thousand years, but still it only signifies a long period of time, unbelievably long compared with an average lifespan of a human being. This span of time (of ascending to God) is seen by humans as 'far off', but is seen as 'near' by God (Surah 70:6 and 7, respectively).

This 'Order, Command or Affair' in the heavens and the earth has been mentioned widely in the Qur'an, in the singular and plural (for example, in Surahs 2:210, 3:83, 3:109, 8:44, 11:23, 22:76, 35:4 and 57:5), stressing that all will return to God. Some of this Order or Affair is non-voluntary and pertains to the system (the universe) and its management, for all forms of matter (Surah 17:44, see above) and angels (Surah 2:30). And some of this Order is voluntary and pertains to human deliberations connected with consciousness. Thus humans and their deliberations may move towards God willingly in body and spirit, or they may be returned to God involuntarily in body but rebelling spiritually.

Taking into consideration what was said about *fitratu Allah* earlier and its connotation of being a born quality (the birth of something conceived earlier) whether in humans or in the universe, one gets the impression that the whole universe was born and is now evolving on its way back towards the source. As everything in the creation 'swims intensively' in gratitude towards God, this implies that the connection to the source was never severed and the whole system is somehow attached to God.

The Day of Judgement

This is one of the most mentioned concepts in the Qur'an. It is the final step in the overall plan. The judgement pertains to the conscious deliberations of mankind. It forms one of the pillars of the message preached by Muhammad. We have already come across it in the quotations cited above. Before judgement takes place, humans will be resurrected. This concept met with much disbelief and astonishment, as can be gathered from the many verses in the Qur'an dealing with this topic. A few more examples are given:

> And the human being says: what! when I am dead shall I then be brought forth alive? But does not the human being bear in mind that We created him aforetime when he was nothing?
>
> (Surah 19:66–67)

And they say, after we will have become bones and dust, shall we really be raised up in a new creation? Say [O Muhammad]: You will be raised from the dead even though you be stones or iron, or some creation yet more monstrous in your minds. Then they will say: Who will bring us back? Say: He who originated you the first time. Then they will shake their heads at you and they will say: When will it be? Say: it may well be soon; on the day when He will call you and you will answer praising Him and you will think you have tarried but a little while.

(Surah 17:49–52)

It is He who has multiplied (scattered) you in the earth; and unto Him you shall be assembled. It is He who causes life and causes death, and to Him belongs the alternation of night and day; what! will you not use your reason?

No, they say what the ancients said before them: what! when we are dead and become dust and bones, shall we indeed be raised up? This, we have been promised before, we and our fathers. This is naught but the fairy-tales of the ancients.

(Surah 23:79–83)

In Surah 82 quoted earlier, it is said that on the Day of Judgement, 'no person shall be of the least avail to another, for on that day all authority shall belong to God'. In Surah 14:48 it says: 'Upon that day the earth shall be changed into a different earth as shall be the heavens, and when they (mankind) shall stand before God, the Omnipotent.' Upon that day, Surah 16:111 says: 'Every person will come disputing on his/her own behalf, and every person shall be paid in full for what he/she did and they shall not be wronged.'

A final quotation comes from Surah 18:47–49:

And [bear in mind] the day when we shall set the mountains in motion, and you shall see the earth void and bare, and We will gather them (mankind) together leaving out none of them. And they shall be presented before your Lord in ranks, [and He will say to them]: you have come unto us [in a lonely state] as We created you upon the first time.

Yes, you thought We would not make good the promise made to you to meet [Us]. And the record [of everyone's deeds] will be laid open and you shall see the sinners

dismayed at the contents. They will say: woe to us. What a
record is this! It leaves out nothing, be it small or great,
but it has counted it. They will find all that they did,
placed before them; and your Lord shall not wrong anyone.

It is important to note that God does not interfere directly in
this life in human affairs, regardless of how much ingratitude the
evildoers will show. In fact, the Qur'an tells us that the unbelievers
were challenging Muhammad to bring all the punishments
promised to fall upon them, to come instantly in this lifetime. This
is clear from the following verses (Surah 6:57–58):

Say [Muhammad]: I [act] upon clear signs from my Lord
but you treated them as lies. That [punishment] which you
desire to be hastened is not in my power; judgement is
with God only. He relates the truth and He is the best of
arbiters. Say: if what you seek to hasten were with me (i.e.,
within my power), the matter between you and me would
have been decided. But God knows best the evildoers.

Surah 18:58 says:

And your Lord is forgiving full of mercy. Were He to take
them to task for that they have earned, He would hasten
for them the chastisement. But no, they have a term (an
appointed time) from which they have no escape.

Surah 16:61 says:

Now if God were to take humans [immediately] to task for
all the evil that they do [on earth], He would not leave on
the earth a single living creature upon its face; but He is
deferring them to a term stated; and when their time arrives they cannot delay it nor can they hasten it, by a single
moment.

Surah 35:45 says:

Now if God were to take humans [at once] to task for
whatever [wrong] they commit [on earth], He would not
leave a single living creature upon its surface. However, He
is deferring them to a term stated [by Him]; and when

their term comes to an end, then they shall realise that God has in His sight all His creatures (servants).

In Surah 86:13–17, Muhammad is being addressed:

> Indeed, this message cuts between truth and falsehood and is no idle tale. Behold, they [who reject it] devise many a false argument [to disprove its truth]; but I shall bring all their scheming to nought. Let, then, the deniers of the truth have their will; let them have their will for a little while.

Finally, I should point out that even Muhammad was getting anxious about whether the promised punishment of those rejecters of the truth would come during his lifetime or after his death, as can be seen from Surah 13:40:

> But whether We let you see [in your life-time, O Muhammad, the fulfilment of] some of what We have promised them, or whether We cause you to die [before the fulfilment], your duty is no more than to deliver the message. It is for Us to do the reckoning.

It is very clear that the punishment of God promised to the evildoers is carried out at the Day of Judgement. Any disasters happening to peoples or individuals have natural causes (that is, created causes) due to processes of natural laws. Therefore they are used in the Qur'an as pointers or indicators which ought to be considered and thought about just like the other phenomena the Qur'an points out.

This, in essence, is telling us that the rise and fall of civilisations and the flourishing and decadence of societies are governed by, and due to, natural laws, which ought to be sought out. Whether the causes are physical (exposure to sandstorms, flooding, and so on) or sociological and political (oppression, imbalance in the distribution of wealth, or any other social disease originating from excessive following of selfish desires), the Qur'an tells us that their study is essential in order to learn the lessons from them. The results of the actions of such natural phenomena are often couched in religious idioms, giving the impression that God interfered directly to give instantaneous judgement. This sort of language has already been discussed above. It must be emphasised that the responsibility for rectifying a wrong done by man against man or nation against nation, or for disasters which are not manmade, falls upon mankind in this life.

In this life, the human being is in full control and is completely responsible for his conduct and management of the affairs of this life. This has already been discussed in detail earlier on in this work. This emphasises the importance of adopting the right concept of God by humanity, since it is from God the concept of justice is derived.

6

DESCRIPTIVE LANGUAGE
OF THE QUR'AN

The Qur'an deals with two worlds, the natural world we live in, and the Other world starting at the Resurrection Day. The Qur'an calls the natural world the witnessable world, because we can observe it. This is the created world of which we are part. Human language is based on our observations of the world we live in, the natural world.

The Other world the Qur'an calls the Absent or Unwitnessable world (often translated as the unseen or hidden world), because we are not part of it and therefore we cannot observe. Thus all the descriptions of the Other world must, by necessity, be rhetorical or allegorical. The Qur'an called attention to both of these aspects. Addressing Muhammad, Surah 3:7 says:

> He it is who has sent down to you the Book, wherein messages (verses) are clear and precise – these are the basis (essence, foundation, literally: mother) of the Book – and others are figurative. But they whose hearts are given to deviation, follow its figures, craving discord, craving an interpretation; yet none knows its interpretation but God. And the stable in knowledge say, 'We believe in it: it is all from our Lord'; yet none will bear this in mind but those who are endowed with insight.

The knowledgeable people, according to the Qur'an, accept and acknowledge the inevitability of using the language of the natural world to describe the Other world, without going into circular arguments, knowing it is figurative.

The allegorical language also applies to descriptions of God, since by definition of the Qur'an (Surah 112), God is outside our language as there is nothing equivalent to Him. This is stressed also in Surah 6:103 in a slightly different manner. The other aspect of describing the Other world is the rhetorical one which pertains to punishment in Hell or the rewarding in Paradise. There are in the Qur'an terrifying descriptions of Hell which are used explicitly for the purposes of frightening readers. For example, in Surah 39:16: 'Above them there shall be sheets of fire and sheets of fire beneath them. In this way does God frighten His creatures (servants). O you creatures of Mine, be then conscious of Me.' In Surah 74:31 it is said: '[Hell] is a great reminder to humans.'

In Surah 74:35 it is described as one of the great forewarnings to humans, irrespective of whether one has chosen to follow (go forward) or to disregard (lag behind) the divine call (Surah 74:36). Having said this, the language used is not all bluff. This brings us back to our starting point about the use of the language of this world to describe something out of this world which is completely beyond our imagination. As terrifying descriptions of Hell have been used to frighten humans away from the evil ways, so luxurious descriptions of Paradise (relative to the audience at that time and place) have been used to draw humans towards the way of God.

7

GOD THROWS THE ROPE AND KEEPS THE DOOR OPEN

We have already discussed the overall plan of the Qur'an for life in this world. The plan involved the devolution of authority to mankind, equipping people with the necessary tools, and putting at their disposal God's creation to utilise during their mandate. It indicated the right way towards God and warned of the consequences of following the excesses of the desires (lusts). It offered freedom to choose a way, asked mankind to vie with each other in doing good works and told them that all will be raised from the dead and judged according to their conduct in their lifetime in this world.

The plan emphasises human responsibility for their actions during their lifetime, and stresses that judgement will be based on one's conduct. This raises two important points. The first point concerns the impression that man is completely left on his own in this life; in other words God is no longer available to mankind during this life. The second point concerns those humans who committed excesses against themselves by following the way of excessive desires and who thus will have accumulated a lot of negative equity when they come to face Judgement Day.

Concerning the first point, God has installed a permanent non-material element or bond between Him and each human being. This linkage is available continuously throughout one's lifetime. It is like a rope attached to a person linking him to God, which he can pull on to get out of danger to safety. It is a non-material bond, which can be activated by humans in a way that something flows across this link between themselves and God. When it is activated by a person, it does not involve getting God to do man's work on earth. Rather, it is like opening a gate and seeing things in a new light, which enables the person involved to act accordingly. It is to be noted that prayers (which need not be publicly announced) serve only as a psychological preparation prior to the activation process. That the human being is the one who works to achieve the desired change is stressed in Surah 13:11. This says: 'Verily, God will not change a people's lot (condition) until they have changed what is in their inner selves (hearts).'

Note the dependence of the 'religious idiom' in the first part, which gives the impression that God directly intervenes to effect the required change, on the natural language in the second part of the statement. Such linkage has already been pointed out in previous chapters, and serves to smooth the transition from the inherited idiom of religious discourse towards the natural rational one.

This activation (of the bond between the human being and God) occurs at various levels of knowledge depending on the experience of the person involved. Hence, every person is capable of seeing in a light commensurate with his/her experience. Whatever the level one starts with, clarity of mind and hard work must be applied: observing, considering and reflecting upon some creation of God, large or small, physical or otherwise.

Concerning those who see the light late in life and who think it is too late for them, the gate to the road towards God is not closed in their faces; rather, they are encouraged to follow it before it is too late. God instructs Muhammad in the Qur'an:

> Say: [Thus speaks God] O you creatures (servants) of Mine who committed excesses against your own selves, do not despair of God's mercy, for God forgives all sins. It is He who is the forgiving One, the Merciful. Hence, turn towards your Lord and submit [your faces, direction] unto Him before the suffering [of death and resurrection] comes upon you, for then you will not be helped.
>
> (Surah 39:53–54)

Reading the Qur'an, one gets the certainty that God will not wrong human beings on Judgement Day, but other than that we cannot circumscribe God's actions; after all, He is Sovereign Subjectivity, as is clear from Surah 21:23: 'He is not accountable [to any one] for what He does, but He questions others for what they do.'

APPENDIX

Surah 30

First of all I must draw the attention of the reader to the point that, unlike the earlier quotations of Qur'anic units in the text where we gave only the first and the last numbers of the verses, in this surah all the numbers are given in accordance with the standard Arabic text. It is clear from the position of the numbers 2, 3 and 4 that a number occasionally falls in the middle of a sentence and not at the end. This is why we avoided the full numbering in the earlier quotations.

This is a comparatively medium-sized surah, which provides a further illustration of the structure of a typical Qur'anic surah and shows the complex interwoven character of the preaching units and the repetitive aspect of pointing to the various signs of God, physical or otherwise. This surah is also one of twenty-nine surahs in the Qur'an which start with single letters of the alphabet, standing singly, not forming a word. In this surah these letters are 'A', 'L', and 'M', usually pronounced on recitation as: alef, lam, mim, respectively. This phenomenon has been explained as an abstract form of a sign of God, pointing to the learning process of writing and reading which characterises human activity.

After the single letters, a political event is mentioned in what appears to be a prediction but which was earlier interpreted as a hope. This is then followed by stressing that the Order (Command) [of this universe] is God's, in the past and in the future. On that [hopeful] day, the believers shall rejoice in God's help Who gives help to whom He wills. That is God's promise. Some preaching follows, reminding the audience (or readers) amongst other things that God has created the heavens and the earth and all that is between them with the truth and for a stated term. They are told that the demise of earlier civilisations was a result of their actions and not due to God's injustice. This is followed by stressing that mankind will be returned to God, and believers in, and deniers of, the truth will be judged and receive their respective dues.

Then a series of 'signs' of God are marshalled as pointers towards God which should be considered and reflected upon. This is followed by preaching, emphasising again that God, who created man in the first instance, will bring him to life again after his death. Then we meet verses addressed to Muhammad personally about the difficulties he was facing in discharging his mission. Muhammad is told to set his direction (face) inclining to the religion (way), as that is God's original creation upon which He disposed mankind, and not to be unsettled. Again we see in this surah, as in many other surahs, that righteous work is associated with expending some of what one cherishes on various categories of causes and that denial of the truth is connected with following one's excessive selfish desires or lust. We also meet an urging to avoid usury and are told that it is better in the sight of God to give *zakat*, the wealth purification dues.

Surah 30

A. L. M.(1) The Byzantians have been defeated(2) in near part of the land, but after their defeat they will be the victors(3) in a few years. With God belongs the Command (Order), first and last. And on that day the believers shall rejoice(4) in God's help; God helps whomsoever He wills, and He is the Mighty, the Merciful.(5) [This is] God's promise. God does not fail His promise but most people do not know it.(6) They know an outward part of the present life but of the hereafter they are unaware.(7)

What! have they not pondered within their own minds (within themselves) that God has not created the heavens and the earth and all that is between them save for a serious end and for a stated term? Yet there are many people who deny that they will ever meet their Lord.(8) What! have they never journeyed in the land and observed how was the end of those who were before them? They were stronger than themselves in might, they broke up the land and built upon it more than they themselves ever built; and their messengers came to them with clear signs. And it was not God who would wrong them, but they wronged themselves.(9) Then evil was the end of evil doers, because they had treated our messages as lies and laughed them to scorn.(10)

God originates creation in the first instance and then brings it back again and unto Him you shall be returned.(11) And on the day when the Hour shall come the wrongdoers will be speechless with despair (confounded);(12) no intercessors shall they have among their associates, indeed they themselves will be denying their associates.(13) And on that day when the Hour shall come they will be sorted out.(14) As for those who believed and did righteous works they shall be made happy in a garden of delight.(15) But as for those who denied the truth and treated our messages as lies, they shall be given to the torment.(16) Extol, then, God when you enter upon the evening hours, and when you rise at the morn.(17) His is the praise in the heavens and the earth and at twilight and at noon.(18) He brings forth the living out of the dead and brings forth the dead out of the living, and He gives life to the earth after it has been dead and likewise you shall be brought forth.(19)

And of His signs is that He created you out of dust and lo, you are humans spreading yourselves everywhere.(20) And of His signs is that He created for you, of yourselves, spouses, so that you might repose in them and He has set between you love (affection) and mercy. Surely there are signs in this for people who reflect.(21) And of His signs are the creations of the heavens and the earth and the variety in your tongues and colour. Surely in that are signs for those who are knowledgeable.(22) And of His signs is your sleep at night or in daytime and your seeking some of His bounties. Surely in that are signs for people who hear.(23)

And of His signs: He shows you the lightning, a source of awe and hope, and He sends down out of the sky water and He revives the earth after its death. Surely in that are signs for people who use reason.(24) And of His signs is that the heavens and the earth stand firm at His bidding; then when He calls you once and suddenly, out of the earth, lo you shall come forth [for Judgement].(25) To Him belongs whatever in the heavens and the earth, all are devoutly obedient to Him.(26) And it is He who creates [all life] in the first instance and brings it forth anew and most easy is for Him, since His is the essence of all that is sublime in the heavens and on earth; and He is the Mighty the Wise.(27)

He strikes for you an example drawn from your own life. Do you have some of those whom your hand possess as [fully-fledged] partners in whatever We may have bestowed upon you as sustenance so that you [and they] would have equal shares in it, and you would fear them just as you might fear [the more powerful of] your equals? So We distinguish the signs for a people who use reason.(28) Nay, but the evildoers follow their own desire without knowledge. And who could guide those whom God has [thus] let go astray, and who [thereupon] have none to help them?(29)

So set your face firmly [O Muhammad], inclining towards the religion, God's original creation upon which He originated (initiated or disposed) mankind. There is no changing God's creation. That is the right religion but most people do not know.(30) [And be you] turning to Him and be conscious of Him and perform the prayers and be not of the idolaters(31) or among those who have split their religion into sects and became partisans where every party rejoicing in what is theirs.(32)

When some affliction touches mankind, they call unto their Lord turning to Him; then when He gives them a taste of mercy lo, a party of them assign associates to their Lord,(33) showing no gratitude for what We gave them. Enjoy yourselves then, but in the end you shall know.(34) Or have We sent down to them any mandate which speaks [in favour] of what they associate with God?(35) And when We let human beings taste mercy, they rejoice in it; but if for that which their hands have forwarded, evil befalls them, behold they despair.(36) Have they not observed that God outspreads and straitens His provisions to whom He wills? Surely in that are signs for a people who will believe.(37) Hence give the kinsman his due (right) and the needy and the wayfarer, this will be best for those who seek the face of God, and those are the prosperous.(38)

And [remember] whatever you may give out in usury that it may increase upon the people's wealth, increases not with God; whereas whatever you pay out in purification dues (*zakat*) seeking God's face, those: they receive recompense manifold.(39) It is God who created you and then has provided you with sustenance, then will cause you to die, then will bring you to life; Can any of your [God] partners do any of these things? Glory to Him! High be He exalted above that they associate.(40) Corruption has appeared in the land and sea as a result of what men's hands have wrought, that He may let them taste [the evil of] some of their doings, so that they might return [to the right way].(41)

Say: Journey through the earth (or land) and behold what happened in the end to those who lived before [you]: most of them worshipped false gods.(42) So set your face towards the right religion before there comes a day from God that cannot be turned back; on that day they shall be sundered apart.(43) He who has denied the truth (disbelieved) will have to bear [the burden of] his denial; and those who have worked righteous deeds they have made goodly provisions for themselves,(44) so that He might reward those who believed and did righteous deeds of His bounty; verily He does not love those who deny the truth.(45)

And of His signs is that He sends the winds with glad tidings [of rain] both that He may cause you to taste His mercy, and that ships may sail at His behest, and so that you may seek His bounty, and you might have cause to be thankful.(46) We have sent before you apostles to their peoples and they brought clear signs and then [by causing the believers to triumph] We inflicted Our retributions upon those who [deliberately] did evil: for We have willed upon Ourselves to help the believers.(47)

It is God who sends the winds that stir the clouds where upon He spreads them in the sky as He wills and causes them to break up so that you can see the rain issuing from the midst thereof. And when He sends it down on such of His creatures (servants) as He wills, lo, they rejoice,(48) though before its coming down upon them, they abandoned all hope.(49) So behold the marks of God's mercy, how He quickens the earth after it was dead; surely He is the quickener of the dead, for to all things His might is equal.(50) Yet if We let on them a wind and they saw it yellow (because of a sand storm) they would have after its coming returned to unbelief.(51)

[O Muhammad] You cannot make the dead hear you, nor can you make the deaf to hear the call when they turn about retreating;(52) and you cannot lead the blind out of their error. None shall give ear to you except those who believe in Our signs and so submit [their direction towards Us].(53) It is God who has created you in weakness, then after weakness has given you strength; then after strength, [old age] weakness and grey hair; He creates what He wills and He is the all-knowing all-mighty.(54) On the day when the Hour strikes, the wrongdoers will swear that they had stayed away but one hour; thus are they ever deceived.(55) But those who were given knowledge and faith will say: you stayed away in God's Book (i.e., as God ordained) till the Day of the Uprising, and this the Day of the Resurrection: but you, you were determined not to know it.(56)

So on that day, the evildoers' excuses will not profit them, nor shall they be asked to make amends.(57) Indeed We have struck in this Qur'an, for mankind, all kinds of similitude, and if you bring them a sign, those who disbelieved will certainly say: you are but making false claims.(58) It is thus that God seals the hearts of those who do not [want to] know [the truth].(59) Therefore have patience [Muhammad], surely God's promise is true and let not those who have no firm belief unsettle you.(60)

NOTES

1 THE QUEST FOR UNDERSTANDING OUR WORLD

1 See the interesting discussion by N. Forsythe in *The Old Enemy*, Princeton, NJ: Princeton University Press, 1987.

2 J. Hick, *An Interpretation of Religion*, London: Macmillan, 1989, pp. 21–33.

3 Quoted in T.R. Glover, *The Conflict of Religions in the Early Roman Empire*, 10th edn, London: Methuen, 1923, p. 91.

4 A. Guillaume, *Prophecy and Divination Among the Hebrews and Other Semites*, London: Hodder & Stoughton, 1938.

5 G.A. Barton, *Semitic and Hamitic Origins*, Philadelphia: University of Pennsylvania, 1934.

6 W.R. Smith, *Lectures on the Religion of the Semites*, 3rd edn, introduction and additional notes by S.A. Cook, London: A. & C. Black, 1927.

7 Such examples can be found in:
- B. Albrektoon, *History of the Gods*, Lund: CWK GLEERUP, 1967.
- H. Ringgren, *Religions of the Ancient Near East*, London: SPCK, 1973.
- J.B. Pritchard, *Ancient Near Eastern Texts Relating to the Old Testament*, 2nd edn, Princeton, NJ: Princeton University Press, 1955.
- W. Beyerlin (ed.) in collaboration with: H. Brunner, H. Schmokel, C. Kuhne, K.-H. Bernhardt and E. Lipinsky; trans. J. Bowden, *Near Eastern Religious Texts Relating to the Old Testament*, London: SCM, 1978.
- A.H. Armstrong (ed.) *Classical Mediterranean Spirituality*, London: SCM Press, 1986.
- Glover, *The Conflict of Religions in the Early Roman Empire*.
- T. Jacobsen, *The Treasures of Darkness*, New Haven, CN: Yale University Press, 1976.

8 J.W. Griffiths, 'The Faith of the Pharaonic Period', in A.H. Armstrong (ed.) *Classical Mediterranean Spirituality*, London: SCM Press, 1986, pp. 3–38.

9 K. Corrigan, 'Body and Soul in Ancient Religious Experience', in A.H. Armstrong (ed.) *Classical Mediterranean Spirituality*, London: SCM Press, 1986, p. 361.

10 Armstrong, pp. 74–6.

11 Griffiths, pp. 3–38.

12 G. Gnoli, 'Zoroastrianism', in M. Eliade (ed.) *The Encyclopedia of Religion*, New York: Macmillan, vol. 15, pp. 579–91.

13 ibid.

14 K. Ward, *Religion and Revelation*, Oxford: Oxford University Press, 1994, p. 329.

15 N. Smart, *The World Religions*, Cambridge: Cambridge University Press, 1989, p. 231.

16 Armstrong, pp. 98–100.

17 Jacobsen, p. 234.

18 ibid., p. 231.

19 Beyerlin, pp. 237–9. It is of interest to note here that the god Chamosh of Mesha of the ninth century BCE is the god Kamish of Ebla of the middle of the third millennium BCE.

20 See the many articles in Armstrong.

21 A.A. Long, 'Epicurians and Stoics', in A.H. Armstrong (ed.) *Classical Mediterranean Spirituality*, London: SCM Press, 1986, pp. 135–53.

22 Ward, p. 98.

23 P. Atherton, 'Aristotle', in A.H. Armstrong (ed.) *Classical Mediterranean Spirituality*, London: SCM Press, 1986, pp. 121–34, especially p. 122.

24 J.P. Kenney, 'Monotheistic and Polytheistic Elements', in A.H. Armstrong (ed.) *Classical Mediterranean Spirituality*, London: SCM Press, 1986, pp. 269–92.

25 R.T. Wallis, 'The Spiritual Importance of Not Knowing', in A.H. Armstrong (ed.) *Classical Mediterranean Spirituality*, London: SCM Press, 1986, pp. 460–80.

26 Ringgren, p. 52.

27 J.C. De Moor, *Anthology of Religious Texts from Ugarit*, Leiden: Brill, 1987. It is clear that the nominative case ending was applied also to the wife of *el*, i.e. Atheratu (equivalent to the customary spelling 'Asheratu').

28 Griffiths, p. 21.

29 B.W. Anderson, *The Living World of the Old Testament*, 4th edn, New Haven, CN: Yale University Press, 1988, p. 280. Here Anderson is quoting T.J. Meek, *Hebrew Origins*, New York: Harper, 1960, p. 169.

30 M. Smith, *Palestinian Parties and Politics that Shaped the Old Testament*, London: SCM Press, 1987.

31 Anderson, p. 155. Anderson says: 'These independent units of tradition [of non-Israelite origin] were not just borrowed … they were appropri-ated, for Israel made them its own by baptising them into the Yahweh faith.'

32 D.B. Redford, *Egypt, Canaan, and Israel in Ancient Times*, Princeton, NJ: Princeton University Press, 1992, p. 422. Again this author also talks of appropriation of old Semitic narratives by the Israelites, especially the Exodus theme.

33 H.W.F. Saggs, *The Encounter with the Divine in Mesopotamia and Israel*, London: The Athlone Press, 1978, pp. 36–40.

34 T.L. Thompson, *The Early History of the Israelite People: From the Written and Archeological Sources*, Leiden: Brill, 1992, pp. 415–23.
35 G. Garbini, *History and Ideology in Ancient Israel*, London: SCM Press, 1988, Chapter 7.
36 H.M. Orlinsky, 'Nationalism-Universalism and Internationalism in Ancient Israel', in H.T. Frank and W.L. Reed (eds) *Translating and Understanding the Old Testament*, Nashville and New York: Abingdon Press, 1970, pp. 206–35. Orlinsky drew attention to the widespread practice of Christian theologians who tend to select a slogan or a quotation from the Hebrew Bible out of context in order to show that its message is universal.
37 Anderson, p. 605.
38 M. Smith, *Yahweh and Other Deities in Ancient Israel*, San Francisco: Harper, 1990.
39 Redford, p. 168, note 192.
40 P.R. Davies, *In Search of Ancient Israel*, Sheffield: Sheffield Academic Press, 1995.
41 J.C.L. Gibson, *Canaanite Myths and Legends*, second edition, Edinburgh: T. and T. Clark Ltd, 1978; Beyerlin, pp. 187–201. Gibson, p. 8, note 1 pointed to the evolution of the use of the term Zephon from being a name of a holy Mount to becoming a designation of a geographical direction later in Hebrew to mean 'north'; however this meaning 'north', for Zephon does not occur in Ugaritic. In this connection, compare Psalm 48:3 and Isaiah 14:13.
42 Exodus 4:22–23; Jeremiah 31:9, etc.
43 J.A. Soggin, *A History of Israel*, London: SCM Press, 1985, under the Mernaptah stele.
44 F. Hommel, *The Ancient Hebrew Tradition*, London; The Society for Promoting Christian Knowledge, 1897, p. 228.
45 G.W. Ahlstrom, *Who Were the Israelites?*, Winona Lake, IN: Eisenbraums, 1986, p. 66.
46 Thompson, p. 311.
47 For a full discussion of the literature on the position of Asherah *vis-à-vis* the cult of Yhwh, see the monograph by S.M. Olyan, *Asherah and the Cult of Yahweh in Israel*, London: The Society of Biblical Literature, 1988.
48 O. Margalith, 'The Origin of the Name Israel', *Zeitschrift für die Alttestamentlische Wissenschaft*, 1990, vol. 102, pp. 225–37.
49 N.P. Lemche, *The Canaanites and Their Land*, Sheffield: Sheffield Academic Press, 1991.
50 ibid., p. 154. See also the discussion in Davies, pp. 52–4, 85.
51 Anderson, p. 641.
52 E. Pagels, *The Gnostic Scriptures*, London: Weidenfeld & Nicolson, 1979.
53 B. Layton,*TheGnostic Scriptures*,London: SCMPress,1987,pp. 376–9.
54 B.L. Mack, *The Lost Gospel*, Dorset: Element Books, 1994.
55 See the symposium on the Nabataeans in *ARAM Periodical*, 1990, vol. 2, nos 1–2.
56 I. Shahid, *Rome and the Arabs*, Washington, DC: Dumbarton Oaks, 1984, Chapter 1.
57 G.W. Bowersock, *Roman Arabia*, Cambridge, MA: Harvard University Press, 1994.
58 Barton, p. 214.

59 I. Browning, *Petra*, London: Chatto & Windus, 1982, p. 44.
60 Beyerlin, pp. 236–40. Mount Nebo appears to have been used as a sanctuary for Yhwh.
61 Davies, p. 68, where Yhwh is reported to be associated with Teman.
62 F.V. Winnett and W.L. Reed, *Ancient Records from North Arabia*, Toronto: University of Toronto Press, 1970, pp. 34, 170–2.
63 D.N. Freedman, '"Who Is Like Thee Among The Gods?" The Religion of Early Israel', in P.D. Miller, Jr, P.D. Hanson and S.D. McBride (eds) *Ancient Israelite Religion: Essays in Honour of Frank Moore Cross*, Philadelphia: Fortress Press, 1987, pp. 315–35. See also Guillaume, p. 316.
64 Barton, Chapter 7.
65 Exodus 4:22–23; Jeremiah 31:9, etc.
66 Isaiah 7:14, 9:6, etc.
67 See for example Barton.
68 See for example Olyan, pp. 23–37, and Garbini, p. 59.
69 A. Deissmann, *Light from the Ancient East: The New Testament Illustrated by Recently Discovered Texts of the Greco-Roman World*, trans. L.R.M. Strachan, London: Hodder & Stoughton, 1912.
70 E. Pagels, *The Origin of Satan*, Princeton: Princeton University Press, 1996, p. 74.
71 R.H. Charles (ed.) *The Apocrypha and Pseudepigrapha of the Old Testament in English*, Oxford: Oxford University Press, 1913; repr. 1965.
72 J.H. Charlesworth (ed.) *The Old Testament Pseudepigrapha*, Oxford: Oxford University Press, 1984.
73 J.M. Allegro, *The Dead Sea Scrolls*, London: Pelican Books, 1958; J.M. Allegro, *The Dead Sea Scrolls and the Christian Myth*, Devon: Westbridge Books, 1979.
74 Layton.
75 B-Z. Wacholder, *The Dawn of Qumran: The Sectarian Torah and the Teacher of Righteousness*, Cincinnati, OH: Hebrew Union College Press, 1983.
76 *The New Testament Translated into Hebrew out of the Original Greek etc*, London: The Society for Distributing Hebrew Scriptures, n.d.
77 *Eyre and Spottiswoode Study Bible: The Holy Bible, Revised Standard Version*, New York: Harper & Row, 1962.
78 Pagels, pp. 110–16.
79 Layton, pp. 9–21.
80 J.L. Buckley, 'Mandaean Religion', in M. Eliade (ed.) *The Encyclopedia of Religion*, New York: Macmillan, 1987, vol. 9, pp. 150–3.
81 J.J. Buckley, 'Ginza', in M. Eliade (ed.) *The Encyclopedia of Religion*, New York: Macmillan, 1987, vol. 5, pp. 561–2.
82 G. Gnoli, 'Manichaeaism', in M. Eliade (ed.) *The Encyclopedia of Religion*, New York: Macmillan 1987, vol. 5, pp 161–70.
83 See Gnoli, note 12.
84 ibid., p. 583.
85 N. Smart, *The World Religions*, Cambridge: Cambridge University Press, 1993.
86 T. Fahd, *La Panthéon de L'arabie Centrale A La Veille De L'Hegire*, Paris: Librairie Orientaliste, Paul Geuthner, 1968, pp. 203–37.
87 S. Moscati, *The Semites in Ancient History*, Cardiff: University of Wales Press 1959.
88 Redford, p. 271.

89 G.E. Mendenhall, *The Syllabic Inscriptions from Byblos*, Beirut: American University of Beirut, 1985, pp. 156–7.

90 G.E. Mendenhall, 'The Nature and Purpose of the Abraham Narratives', in P.D. Miller, Jr, P.D. Hanson and S.D. McBride (eds) *Ancient Israelite Religion: Essays in Honour of Frank Moore Cross*, Philadelphia: Fortress Press, 1987, pp. 352–3.

2 INTERPRETATION OF THE CONCEPTS 'RELIGION' AND 'REVELATION'

1 W.C. Smith, *The Meaning and End of Religion: A New Approach to the Religious Traditions of Mankind*, New York: The New American Library, 1963.
2 ibid., p. 192, n. 35a.
3 ibid., pp.198–9, n. 58.
4 ibid., p. 34.
5 ibid., p. 80.
6 L. Gardet, *Encyclopedia of Islam*, Leiden: Brill, vol. 2, 1965, pp. 293–6. The author rebutted the idea that the term *deen* is originally Persian, as was suggested in previous studies quoted in the first edition of this encyclopedia, namely those of Noldeke and Vollers.
7 G. Buccellati, *Ebla and the Amorites*, in *Eblaitica*, vol. 3, ed. C.H. Gordon and G.A. Rendsburg, Winona Lake, IN: Eisenbrauns, 1992.
8 P. Byrne, *Natural Religion and the Nature of Religion: The Legacy of Deism*, London: Routledge, 1989.
9 D. Dennett, *Darwin's Dangerous Idea: Evolution and the Meaning of Life*, London: Allen Lane, 1995, p. 141.
10 See the contribution of Colin Gunton, pp. 147–62, and that of Don Cupitt, pp. 247–52, in R. Gill (ed.) *Readings in Modern Theology*, London: SPCK, 1995.
11 See the comments of Roger Penrose in *The Shadow of the Mind*, Oxford: Oxford University Press, 1994, p. 420.
12 K. Ward, *Religion and Revelation*, Oxford: Oxford University Press, 1994.
13 ibid., pp. 16, 340.
14 ibid., p. 91.
15 ibid., p. 110.
16 ibid., p. 193.
17 G. Garbini, *History and Ideology in Ancient Israel*, London: SCM Press, 1988, pp. 21–32.
18 J. Maxwell Miller and J.H. Hayes, *A History of Ancient Israel and Judah*, London: SCM Press, 1986, p. 78.
19 D.B. Redford, *Egypt, Canaan, and Israel in Ancient Times*, Princeton, NJ: Princeton University Press, 1992, p. 422.
20 ibid., p. 422.
21 Ward, pp. 90–1.
22 H.W.F. Saggs, *The Encounter with the Divine in Mesopotamia and Israel*, London: The Athlone Press, 1978, p. 37.
23 R. Gill (ed.) *Readings in Modern Theology*, London: SPCK, 1995.
24 Ward, p. 228.

4 A CROSS-SECTION OF THE QUR'AN

1 The translations used are:
- A. Y. Ali, *The Meaning of the Holy Qur'an*, Baltimore, MD: Amana Corporation, 1991.
- A. Arberry, *The Koran Interpreted*, Oxford: Oxford University Press, 1964.
- M. Asad, *The Message of the Qur'an*, Gibraltar: Dar Al Andalus, 1980.
- N.J. Dawood, *The Koran*, London: Penguin Books, 1993.
- J.M. Rodwell, *The Koran*, London: Everyman's Library, 1992.

2 J. Penrice, *A Dictionary and Glossary of the Koran*, New Delhi: Cosmo Publications, 1978.
3 G. Monnott, '*Salaat*', in *Encyclopedia of Islam*, Leiden: Brill, vol. 8, 1995, pp. 925–35.
4 See Rodwell's translation of the Qur'an, pp. 323–4, n. 3.
5 See for example Hosea 11:1.

5 THE OVERALL PLAN OF THE QUR'AN FOR MANKIND

1 For example, 4Q521 Fragment 1 column 2 line 6, as in the transliteration given by Robert Eisenman and Michael Wise in *The Dead Sea Scrolls Uncovered*, Devon: Element, 1992, p. 91.
2 The original words are quoted in *The Brown–Driver–Briggs Hebrew and English Lexicon*, Peabody, MA: Hendrickson Publishers, 1996, reprinted from the 1906 edition (originally published Boston: Houghton, Mifflin).
3 It is interesting to note the use of the verb *fatara* and its derivatives in the Hebrew Bible – especially Exodus 13:2, 13, 15; 34:19 and Numbers 3:12; 8:16; 18:15 – to describe birth of babies from the womb. An analogy is in Proverbs 17:14, where the active participle of *fatara* is used likening the (bursting out) of water in the birth process to the outbreak of disputes.
4 It is worth pointing out that the common everyday usage of *fatara* and its derivatives relates to breaking or cracking. For example, *futoor* means 'breaking fast', whether the fast was voluntary for religious reasons or involuntary due to being asleep at night. The literal implication in this process of breaking fast is 'opening the mouth'. That this usage of this verb and its derivatives in this sense is very old may be seen from its use also in the Hebrew Bible, as in Psalm 22:8 *wa-yafteru bi-shafah*, i.e. they 'broke out' with [their] lips [insults].
5 K.A. Nizami, in D.B Macdonald [H. Haase], '*Djinn*', in the *Encyclopedia of Islam*, 2nd edn, Leiden: Brill, vol. 2, 1965, pp. 546–9.
6 T.R. Glover, *The Conflict of Religions in the Early Roman Empire*, 10th edn, London: Methuen, 1923, p. 15.

INDEX